*This book is dedicated
to past and future Johnson family
members and Johnson directors and
employees who have participated in the
success of Johnson Wax for more than
100 years.*

THE ESSENCE OF A FAMILY ENTERPRISE

Doing Business the Johnson Way

Samuel C. Johnson
Chairman & Chief Executive Officer
S. C. Johnson & Son, Inc.

Cartoons appear by permission of the artists, Don Pegler, Jeff MacNelly, and Jim Whiting.

TABLE OF CONTENTS

Samuel C. Johnson

PREFACE

Centennial celebrations are rare occasions for American businesses, because our society has been marked by so many changes. Those corporations which do succeed for a hundred years or more often publish a history to report their challenges and achievements and to express plans for the future.

This selection of essays has been prepared in reflection upon the S. C. Johnson & Son, Inc. 100th anniversary celebrated in 1986.

As I reflected about the past during our centennial period, and thought about the roles of numerous people in our successes, it became even clearer to me that our family firm operates on a set of principles and philosophies. It also became clear that these principles and philosophies transcend the generations that have gone before and hold true for as far as I can see into the future. With these understandings, it became my goal to reflect on these principles by writing a series of essays which points to the future by drawing on the past.

What I have tried to do is put into words those principles and philosophies which I think will be helpful to future generations of Johnson people, whether they be members of my family or members of the larger Johnson Wax family. It is a book that looks ahead—one that draws on the past but does not dwell on it. The historical examples present throughout are used to make points that might be helpful in future decisions.

As a family enterprise, we have the opportunity to think for the long term. We have said on many occasions that we do not run our business for tomorrow, or the next quarter, or the next year, but for future generations. We can say that and still be credible because we have been a family business for four generations and look forward to being a family business in succeeding generations.

The topics of these essays include employee relations, the value of being a family-controlled firm, research and development and technological advances, advertising and marketing, corporate support of the arts, voluntarism, and worldwide markets. Throughout the essays, the fundamental principles of integrity, loyalty, and striving for excellence are constants.

As a businessman, I believe in doing what we call the "right things." In order to see the right things, we must have a broad perspective,

1

which means the ability to see beyond the immediate. I trust that this effort to reflect on our past and our principles and to present them in a way that can be useful in the future will be a source of information and of inspiration for others, as they decide the future of this or any other firm.

I would like to acknowledge those who helped in the preparation of the manuscript: Thomas B. Martin, retired vice president for public affairs, who conducted all the interviews; his wife, Helen, who transcribed the tapes; E. O. (Jim) Jones, Jr., retired public relations director, who served as researcher and coordinator; Serge E. Logan, director of corporate social responsibility, who edited the transcripts and kept the facts straight; and Dr. Robert A. Scott and Marnia F. Kennon of The Curtis Publishing Company, who guided the final editing and preparation of the essays and production of the book.

THE FAMILY-CONTROLLED FIRM—ITS BENEFITS, ITS CHALLENGES

"The one constant . . . is the family focus on the long-term success of the company."

There are distinct advantages to being a family corporation, especially when you are competing against public firms. Public companies do have some advantages, principally unlimited access to the public equity financial markets and the ability to make acquisitions with stock. Also, in some cases the public market is the only way minority family shareholders can diversify their investments or settle their estates. But the burdens of dealing with thousands of shareholders with diverse expectations as well as a weight of potential takeover encumbers the chief executive officer of virtually every public corporation.

The preeminent edge for a family firm if it is totally private may well be secrecy from your competition, a cherished privilege among private CEOs. You can even liken this to a game of poker. Take a public and a family corporation and say that all things are pretty much equal: they are roughly of the same size, they have comparable market shares for competing products and similar technological expertise. In other words, the cards are being dealt straight.

Now, the private firm can hold each and every one of those cards tight to its vest, right through the betting and until it's time to lay them down. But the public firm has to expose the majority of its cards almost from the start, keeping only a proprietary ace or two until its hand is called. The private company can see many of the strengths and weaknesses of its public competitor and act accordingly. Curiously enough, the private player doesn't even have to show much of its hand when the moment of truth arrives. And if it wins, it simply takes the money off the table, with the public company never really knowing the amount.

Some people assume that public companies represent the

benchmark of better business, that if you want profits to soar, it's best to operate as a public enterprise. But it is difficult to compare earnings between the two.

A public company does its utmost to enhance short-term earnings, numbers that appear in quarterly and annual reports: columns of black ink that keep shareholders happy, content, and quiet. But a family-controlled company manages its earnings from another perspective, with success measured in terms of years and decades, and not merely quarter-by-quarter. It can accept lower earnings in lieu of stiff tax liabilities. Certain tax write-offs are viewed as a long-range opportunity, and not as a drawback. For these and several other reasons, judging the relative performances of public and private firms—given the different arenas in which they function—can produce dubious results.

Logically, one might think public companies would show higher profit margins. But a study of public and private company earnings conducted by the University of Southern California business school—one of the few ever attempted on this matter, since acquiring data on private firms is difficult—concluded that private companies had earnings margins greatly higher than public corporations. The private outfits also earned higher returns on assets.

The game is not, I should stress, intrinsically unfair. Indeed, the combined estimated sales volume of the top fifty private industrial firms would barely crack the top five of the *Fortune* 500. But the hinderances placed on public corporations are also part of the game. When a company is private and not registered with the SEC, it is not compelled to reveal quarterly results, or to produce an annual report, the results of which are published in newspapers. There are no requirements for financial disclosure to any government agency, save for a few exceptions like the state of Massachusetts, where you have to file an abbreviated annual report just for doing business there.

Essentially a private company can conduct its business free from the glare of public scrutiny. Your competitors, moreover, don't know what you're doing. They have little idea of how strong you are, where problems might have arisen, or even if you're winning. They can figure your share of a particular market through Nielsen and SAMI reports, but they don't have the slightest notion of your bottom line. More important, they don't know how other parts of your enterprise affect the company, either positively or negatively. In sum, you are a downright mysterious entity.

I can easily envision competitors like American Home Products trying to guess what Johnson Wax is going to do next. What new products, for instance, we're about to introduce. American Home can see our test markets once the products have hit the store shelves, but they don't know how much we're spending on research or where we're opening new plants abroad. By the time they do recognize what we're up to and attempt to counter, we've established an important head start.

A CEO of a public company is beholden to literally thousands of individuals and interests. His time spent actually managing the business, trying to make money, is cut appreciably. The public CEO must take to the road to pump the company's stock, meeting with security analysts, talking to investment bankers, informing *The Wall Street Journal* reporters and newsmen from local papers.

He must also spend countless hours with government agencies. And when shareholders call to complain about the company's quarterly earnings report—or even to compliment the CEO—he's forced to talk with them. John Batten, Chairman of Twin Disc, has told me that he has spent at least a third of his time speaking with analysts, trying to get people around the country interested in his company's stock.

The outright financial costs of SEC compliance are also high. Indeed, were we totally public, we clearly would be forced to spend hundreds of thousands of dollars every year on legal fees, registration fees, filing requirements, publishing quarterly and annual reports, and so forth. When Congoleum Corporation was public (it went private in 1980) its chairman figured all the requirements of being a public corporation cost his company in the neighborhood of $7 million a year!

A private company also is free from the vagaries of the stock market, ups and downs that sometimes, through no fault of the management, can send shudders through a corporation. How well these fluctuations are accepted depends much on the nature, personality, and common sense of the shareholders. A large number of public shareholders are a more volatile audience than a few members of one's family.

The best situation, in my view, is a private company where the majority of the stock is concentrated in one family member's hands. That individual is therefore free to make the decisions that are in the best long-term interest of the company. If there are periods of poor performance, one hopes the family and employee shareholders are understanding and aware that short-term profits must sometimes be sacrificed for the firm's future health.

A truly public company, where you've got thousands and thousands of shareholders, is a different matter. Most of the time the inside management group has enough control, in that shareholders supportively sign their proxies. The inside managers and board members also control the nomination committees, the agenda of the annual meeting, and so on.

Nonetheless, they do take lumps from dissidents, suffer serious inquisitions if earnings don't meet expectations, and are picked at by security analysts and government agencies, if not taken over by a hostile raider or even one who seems friendly. But most of the time the management endures.

A better scenario is a public company controlled by one or a small group of family or management shareholders, where there is access to the public market for acquisitions or additional capital, but without the fear of internal strife or outside takeovers. The worst situation I can imagine for a CEO is when a company is public, but heavily family-owned, with no more than five percent of the stock concentrated in any member's hands. There you have the disadvantages of public scrutiny and no concentration of control, and not only do you have to argue with Wall Street, but also with uncles, cousins, and nieces. Should the CEO want to open a new plant that is vital for business growth, and the shareholders want higher dividends instead, then the CEO could easily be outvoted.

While we at Johnson are free from the uncertainties of the stock market and the family bickering that's described above, we do care about the value of our stock. Shares are sold to our key executives on a selected basis; a formula regulates the value according to the company's performance. We don't get the huge upward or downward swings that you see in the stock market, but then I genuinely feel that the performance of the company is a better measure of long-term stock value than the psychological enthusiasm of the market.

Family ownership of a private company is usually an advantage over public ownership, provided there is enough concentration of ownership in one or two members. Management of such private organizations can, to be sure, take several forms. Professional management, brought in by the family owners, often best serves a company's interests.

In a family enterprise that does not bring in outside management, one hopes that ownership—and perhaps more important, *control*—is vested in the most talented member of the family. Should this go on for generations, it results in a continuity of management and management's philosophy. When good things are passed along, they gain even more credibility with age. As we have developed our "This We Believe" philosophy over many years, it has become more and more credible. It spans the generations.

Johnson Wax was one of the first companies to institute profit sharing, a practice established by my grandfather. My father initiated a no-layoff policy during the Great Depression of the 1930s. For many years the company has been committed to giving five percent of pre-tax profits to charity. My father followed through with those ideas, as have I. They are by now a strong part of our corporate culture. Our employees are confident that management policy and style will remain the same as they have been over the last five decades.

Not long ago I received a letter from one of our employees, a mechanic I, frankly, had never met, but who had been working for the company for twenty-three years. He said he had been reading about the layoffs at some local companies in the Racine *Journal Times*. "I just felt moved to write you a letter and say 'Thank you' for all the good years that I've had at the company."

I don't believe that kind of feeling is engendered in many public companies. Only in a family business, where even the employees are something of an extended family, does management continuity breed great loyalty. There is always going to be one percent who are dissatisfied no matter what happens. But the other ninety-nine percent believe in the company and its management.

The vast majority of our people *know* we're not going to change direction and abuse them. And in turn, I know I can count on their loyalty. There have been only a couple of times where I've had to go in front of the employees and ask them for exceptional efforts, where I've said, "Honest to God, help us and pitch in." Invariably, they have responded.

They also know that competitive realities require restructuring of certain parts of the company sometimes, and while no one wants to be among those whose jobs have been restructured out, everyone knows that those affected will be treated fairly.

Of course, if the company founder is a miserly and tough old goat, and his disagreeable ways are genetically and psychologically transmitted to the next generation of management, then you're talking about continuity with no redeeming social value. However, when family ownership places a family member in control of a company, and everyone in the firm knows clearly who the boss is, and who will still be the boss five or ten years hence, then there's a palpable air of stability.

Indeed, in S. C. Johnson & Son, Inc., the owner-manager's name is on the building. And this is a plus when it comes to hiring. Since the average tenure of a public CEO is a little more than six years, a skilled, next-level professional manager in search of a secure position can't be sure whom he will be working for several years down the line. A new CEO is likely to change the way a company does its business, making his mark as quickly as possible. Professionals are aware of this. Moreover, they know they could join a public company and be a victim of a takeover and purge a year or two later. But with a private company, it's obvious they can settle into their jobs, work well with top management, use their talents to the fullest, and see a well functioning relationship stay that way.

There's an old and often-repeated scenario that goes like this: the first generation starts the company, the second builds it up, and the third generation *screws it up*. Well, I represent the fourth generation at Johnson, and my father certainly didn't screw it up during his turn.

My great-grandfather, who was in his fifties when he started the company, got the enterprise rolling. My grandfather was really the initial builder; he diversified the fledgling product line of waxes and polishes. My father took a regional manufacturer of waxes and polishes and turned it into an international company. If there is any major contribution I've made, you might say it's in diversifying—expanding the product line even more, into insecticides, personal care products, industrial products, financial, commercial and home services, and expanding foreign operations from eleven to forty-five countries.

It is now obvious to me that every generation of a family business has to bring something new to the enterprise: that is, something that hadn't been thought of by—and beyond the visions of—the previous generations. It has happened in our family and will hopefully happen in the succeeding generations, or we will atrophy on existing products, markets, businesses, and geographic locations.

Not only is it important to the company for the next generations to bring something new to the enterprise, but it is equally important to members of each generation. They will feel the great personal satisfaction that results from being a true contributor of a new dimension to the business in their own right, in spite of those, including members of the family, who prefer the *status quo*.

None of us were clones of our fathers or mothers, in precise management style, in the scope of our ideas, or in any facet of our lives. Yet each of us has built upon what we believed were the positive parts of the family heritage. In a public company, or even a private firm controlled by professional management, a successor is less likely to build on the heritage of someone he just worked for, and may not have liked to boot. Change may be refreshing, but when a company makes radical shifts every five years, with no foundation or consistency, then the organization grows schizophrenic and suffers.

Untalented, misdirected, and poor CEOs of public corporations do not, however, last as long as similar managers in a family company. If the CEO of a public company is doing a terrible job, Wall Street is going to drive him out. The stock will fall so low that someone can come in with a line-up of opposing shareholders' votes at the annual

Taken in 1917, the photograph shows three generations of the Johnson male descendants: Samuel Curtis Johnson (seated), Herbert F. Johnson (right), and H.F. Johnson Jr. (at age 18).

Sam Johnson met with his father in London when he was serving as Vice President and European Regional Director (1961).

meeting and simply chuck him. That is, if the directors don't do it first; it doesn't happen often enough. Strangely, a family corporation can likewise end up placing a family member in control who turns out—putting it mildly—to be incompetent.

This is why I believe that one of the prime requirements for a healthy, family-owned company is to have a very strong and independent board of directors. It should contain members who are well-recognized professionals, high-level business people in their own right; individuals who are not family members. They are a safety valve. Therefore, if I go around the bend the day after tomorrow, and the results begin to show, my independent board could say, "Sam, we think it's time to turn it over to the next generation, or give your seat to professional management until the next generation is properly groomed."

One can't forget that I could in turn just call a special board meeting and fire all the independent directors. But this is unthinkable and would incur the wrath of the rest of the family and the management—not to mention possible lawsuits. Successful boards are rather collegial bodies. If all the directors are family members, or if the managers start fighting like preschoolers, the company is in dire straits. The practical point of the matter is that a CEO/owner simply doesn't fire a group of distinguished citizens, not of the caliber chosen for the board of a successful and respected private company.

However, a family company can reach the point where the lines of succession are not so clear. Our firm has been historically fortunate in that there had been only one logical successor through the generations. (The fact that the stock was concentrated by archaic male chauvinistic or age-biased principles won't hold today, but that— offering no apologies—is how it has been up until now, a situation that, after my tenure is over, may change.) When a strong leader departs, and several fight to take that place, it's obvious how messy the situation can become.

Indeed, one sees this in many non-democratic governments. A dictator is overthrown or dies, and the factions competing in the vacuum of power virtually rip the fabric of the nation. Therefore, in the area of succession, a public company may have the edge on a private, family-managed business. Unless, of course, concentrated control is handed from one individual to another.

This is not the case with the next generation of Johnsons. There are two boys and two girls in our family, and we face the risk of losing that "concentration." But today I can add an important caveat: our business has become diversified, with interests in many areas, from financial services, to chemicals, to commercial services and personal care products. And even though we have several family members who may take leadership roles, I envision no major problems, primarily because of that business diversity. Authority—and in some cases, ownership—can be split along the lines of the greatest talent or interest on the part of our children. While it isn't the easiest trick to manage, it can be done. Johnson Worldwide Associates, as an example, was spun out of the parent and has become a family-controlled, public company.

I don't believe, though, that it's sound to have siblings competing against each other. The malevolent machinations of J.R. and Bobby Ewing, battling for control of the family oil company in the TV series "Dallas," are hyperbolic, but in spirit not that far from the truth. No matter how close-knit a family, there is still a great potential for disagreements.

This can be avoided by spreading authority to various parts of the total operation. Our firm currently has some existing separation of businesses; unit companies each serve as bases of operation, reporting all the way to an executive vice president. There is some sharing of manufacturing facilities, but the system works well. So, should the family need to "break up" the company—either in terms of spheres of management authority or ownership—the structure is already in place. We may take more segments of the company public to allow family shareholders to diversify, to bail out their estate, or to allow that segment to acquire additional companies for stock. In any event family control should prevail.

The sons and daughters of Mr. & Mrs. Johnson, all active in the business, are standing, Curt Johnson, left, and Fisk Johnson; and seated Helen Johnson-Leipold, left, and Winnie Marquart.

In 1975, the company removed all fluorocarbon propellants from its production lines worldwide and added a shield to its aerosol products reassuring consumers that the products can be used with confidence.

The family-controlled firm also has the mechanics to make decisions faster than public corporations. This again goes back to having one person, with clear authority, in charge of each major unit of the company. It's the mark of a well-run family company.

When a public corporation grows large, so inevitably does its bureaucracy. And the red tape that bureaucracies create can often be cut only lengthwise—it stifles and binds. Bureaucracies are also self-perpetuating; they grow like noxious weeds and are difficult to disentrench. I worry about the one we've been developing. Still, unlike the majority of our public competitors, we can move quickly in a crisis. We don't need to go through multiple committees, but can simply bring together the key people and move. The organization has no built-in inertia and is able to implement a course of action swiftly, with the key family owner-manager's support.

In certain circumstances committees can be an advantage. Procter & Gamble has a very elaborate review committee system. It's one of their strengths, and they are about nine times larger than Johnson Wax. But what we lack in size we can make up for in our ability to move quickly on opportunities and problems and to make correct and *timely* decisions.

A good example is our decision in 1975 to take fluorocarbons out of our products. We had done some homework on the matter, but when it became apparent that keeping them in the products would harm our reserve of consumer trust and loyalty, we made the commitment to remove the propellant within a week. Bang. We quickly made a very significant move for the company.

There have been incidents where we have been outraced into a market with a new product, such as lemon-scented furniture polish. Faced with the need to come up with a quick counterpunch, we did so and won that battle. I would have preferred to be the innovator of the lemon idea, but you can't always be the first. Sometimes you have to play catch-up, and it's important to do that as well as being an innovator.

So, speed and action are crucial, something you can't have with eighteen committees reviewing an idea or with a non-creative bureaucracy in the way. In our organization a person with a good idea can get it approved and going much faster, I believe, than in a large public firm.

Lastly, a family corporation can do things of social or cultural value that a public company might be reluctant even to entertain, if only for fear of shareholder fury. Granted, many major public companies give millions of dollars to the humanities, the arts, charity, education, and public television, among other good causes. This has been recognized over the last decade or so as necessary "corporate responsibility."

However, public firms that are about the size of Johnson Wax frequently have shareholders who don't view philanthropy that way. These shareholders don't see funding an art exhibit as anything but a cut from the dividend check. We, on the other hand, can do those things that enhance the communities in which we live and work without having to explain it to thousands and thousands of people, over and over.

Being in a family company compels you to think of the community. One certainly does not want to dump toxic wastes on a site that your children or grandchildren may one day occupy. One is concerned for subsequent generations—the museums they will be able to visit, the schools the children will attend.

We have been strongly supportive, for example, of The Prairie School, a non-profit, coeducational independent day school for students in grades one to twelve, which was the inspiration of my wife, Gene, and her friend, Mrs. Willy Hilpert. They saw a need in our community to augment our respected public school system with a curriculum and a learning environment to develop individual student achievement in a college preparatory program. The result is a successful enterprise that is about to celebrate its 25th anniversary. Gene has not only served on The Prairie School Committee from its inception, but also currently serves as its Chairperson.

This is the type of a project a public company might find difficult to help establish. As a company, we have given that five percent of pre-tax earnings to charitable, cultural, and civic interests for decades, and we'll continue to make that investment in the future, a future that has an importance that transcends the company's business. Hired hands in public corporations may have warm hearts, but the demands of shareholders and Wall Street can indeed be chilling.

As I explained, the private company has an edge over public firms because of secrecy. But this doesn't mean you cloak your operation as if you're in the Kremlin. I read where an official of one private corporation said: "It will be a cold day in hell before [his company] talks to the press." That's ridiculous. A CEO can talk about his businesses without giving away secrets, and the media are part of the community. Isolating oneself and belligerently refusing to become part of the greater public does a disservice to the corporation and the community.

My management style is without a doubt different from that of my father. He might have seen today's business and social climate quite differently than I do. He was more of a gutsy, hands-on, decision maker, while I tend to pick brains, get the best ideas I can from others, resolve on a consensus, and then make up my mind. I think allowing such participative action on the part of more employees gives everyone a better feel for the organization. The thing is, each generation in a family-owned company probably adapts to and creates change, to win in the conditions that are present in the business and society of the day.

The one constant, as I've said, is the family focus on the long-term success of the company, for the next generation and ones even further down the line. It can be said that this is more a matter of pride than success for the family pocketbook. And it's a luxury that public corporations—with all the pressures that being public creates—simply cannot afford.

THE QUALITIES OF LEADERSHIP

*"The able leader gets . . . the maximum horsepower out of the
whole organization. And much of the fine tuning hinges on
communications style."*

It is said that the average tenure of a business leader, a chief
executive who answers to virtually no one but himself, is 6.2 years.
During the course of an average four-decade career, this is a relatively
short time to be at center stage. Moreover, not many experiences that
one acquires as a supervisor, in middle management, or even at the
vice-presidential level truly prepare an executive for the demands and
nuances of leadership.

Indeed, one generally begins a career with a specific skill, be it in
engineering, sales, or finance, or any other. As promotions come
along, however, you are gradually moved farther and farther away
from actually practicing that skill. Eventually, an executive spends very
little time employing his or her original area of expertise, and makes
the transition into leading rather than doing. Still, until the final step is
taken into a chief executive position, it is often difficult to appreciate
what such leadership ultimately entails.

And for most individuals, there is not much time for learning to
lead. With the normal press of business matters, those 6.2 years can
pass quickly. I've been fortunate in that I've been a chief executive
officer for more than twenty years, a period in which I feel I've
learned a few things about the nature of leadership. Curiously
enough, the essential qualities of an effective leader are very simple
and basic. Although some of the qualities that must be developed
clearly run against human nature, there is little mystery to the art.

What is this thing called leadership? Well, in the most basic sense it is
the ability to bring a group of people together into a common and
cooperative course of action. A leader may sometimes have to convince
these people to make temporary personal sacrifices—or put forth
more effort than they really wanted to give, or didn't know they could
give—to achieve a long-range goal. And while that goal may not be
apparent to all, it is up to the leader to articulate the vision, making it

compelling to an individual, a small group, a large organization, or even an entire nation.

Upon the death of President Franklin Roosevelt, journalist Walter Lippmann said, "The final test of a leader is that he leaves behind him in other men the conviction and will to carry on." The genius of a good leader, he added, "is to leave behind him a situation which common sense, without the grace of genius, can deal with successfully." In sum, Lippmann was saying that a good leader builds an organization infused with sound principles and values, indelibly locked into the intellect and soul of all. But how does a leader go about this?

Well, I'm convinced that the primary quality or skill, *the* requisite for any good leader, is the ability to communicate with other people: direct, face-to-face communication. You cannot lead by sitting in an office and thinking productive thoughts. You cannot lead by merely issuing memos. Orders that flow from a remote sanctuary may carry weight and often will be carried out. But such missives fail to spark initiative, trust, or loyalty. It is direction, but it is certainly not leadership.

Leadership, then, is a very personal thing. *You*, the leader, are trying to draw the optimum talent from every person in the organization. These include technical talents, creative talents, and routine talents, all of which are important to business success. The leader must organize these individuals so that they interact with each other in the best possible way, so that they are mutually supportive. The able leader gets, if you will, the maximum horsepower out of the whole organization. And much of the fine tuning hinges on communication style.

While a chief executive's communication style obviously denotes form, as opposed to substance, its impact upon an organization must never be underestimated. In fact, a leader's communication style ultimately has an effect on substance, in that it creates a mood or environment that can temper or spur the workforce. A little humor, for example, goes a long way in nurturing a relaxed and productive environment.

A leader sets a style which after time is often followed throughout the company. There is an old story about a corporate president who came to work with a dab of peanut butter on his chin, a bit of breakfast he'd missed wiping clean. And before you know it everybody in the firm, from the vice president to the stock boy, had dabbed peanut butter on his chin. This is, to be sure, hyperbolic, but there is no question that a leader establishes a company's style.

On the other hand, I don't completely accept the "Organization Man" theory, which proposes that if you have a strong leader, somehow everyone in the company will mold himself into an image of what he thinks the leader wants him to be. To me, this would indicate a failing on the part of a leader. A good manager, with communication, can cleverly create an atmosphere in which creative freedom of expression is encouraged. Indeed, if there is not cross-communication among people of different backgrounds and disciplines, if new ideas and approaches are not proposed and tried, even at the risk of failure, then an organization will grow stagnant.

There is a vast difference between setting a tone and cultivating a mass of clones. A leader who doesn't get this across to his employees, who doesn't encourage creative expression, is doing himself and the organization a disservice. And one can't set a tone without communicating effectively and enthusiastically.

Unfortunately, while communication is such a large part of leadership, we really don't teach it well enough, or early enough, in schools. Once children are past grade school, I believe, a strong interpersonal communications curriculum should be introduced. There are not nearly as many debate teams in junior high and high school as there were thirty and forty years ago. Students should be given ample chance to sharpen their verbal skills. When you look at the natural leaders in the high schools, they are the young men and women who can communicate effectively.

An interview as part of the recruitment process to enter any major graduate business school is essential. Any bright individual can compose a good application, taking the time to polish and rework sentences. A person with a good academic record can create a document that will nearly knock you over. But sit that same individual down and begin talking with him or her, and a different image might emerge. I would ask myself, "Does this individual have a distinctive personality aside from the academic honors?" And, "Is there a sense of humor that will aid this person through the ups and downs of business?" These are vital leadership qualities. However, one doesn't get a feel for these qualities from just an application.

Good communication skills, admittedly, don't always come naturally. I well remember the agony my father would endure before giving his annual profit sharing speeches. He knew that such talks were required by his leadership role, and that once a year he'd have to get up in front of the staff of the entire company. He'd practice the talks on me, reading them aloud over and over.

My father wasn't altogether effective as a public speaker. He was dynamic in small groups, from management committees to one-to-one talks. But in front of large audiences . . . I vowed that I would not go through the same misery he suffered before such meetings, and

H. F. Johnson addresses the annual Profit Sharing Day get-together in the late 1940s in the Great Workroom. His report to all employees each year was an assignment he didn't relish.

decided that I was going to learn how to speak in public. I hadn't learned it at Cornell, and it wasn't taught at the Harvard Business School. But I considered it an important enough art to hire a private speech coach. And the lessons have served me well.

A second major point is that when you communicate, it must be done with complete honesty. I realize this may seem obvious, but it is absolutely essential. A leader cannot hide bad news for long. If you bend the truth once or twice, sooner or later the cover-up is going to catch up with you. If there is good news concerning the company, by all means say it loudly. If there is bad news, well, speaking softly and seriously is fine. But be sure you are totally honest, comprehensive, and are heard.

Total honesty in leadership is simply the right way to do business. Yet there are secondary benefits. If you are honest, then you can retain the confidence that you are never going to be tripped up by a misstatement of the past. Moreover, people can sense when one is being totally honest, which enhances credibility, and people readily see through dishonesty.

I've discussed at length the art of communicating. But equally important to all this is the knack of *listening*! A leader has to be willing to listen, to be sensitive, to hear what other people are saying and, above all, to understand what they are *really* saying. It's a fact that leaders don't always hear the whole story, but are told what others think the leader wants to hear.

My personal decision-making process involves soaking up the best advice I can get from the people I think know the most about a given subject. When I'm confident I've gotten the best advice possible, then I'll make up my mind.

There are leaders, of course, who instinctively know the right decision without going through such a process. There must have been many times on the battlefield when General George Patton didn't give a whit for what anyone else said, and charged off in a direction he knew would lead to victory. And there have been occasions in my life— and in my father's—where the advice has been unanimous to do things one way, and yet we opted for another. The ability to accept the best advice and yet have the courage to ignore it is also a quality of leadership. Leadership sometimes puts one in a position of being alone, out front, as it were, leading.

Another mark of a good leader is rallying those who don't agree with your decision—and getting them to carry it out in a vigorous way. This is a rare quality and has much to do with loyalties built over time. My father had it. Even though he wasn't the gentlest of leaders, he earned a superior loyalty and respect. Because of his instinctive good judgment, a habitual pursuit of excellence, absolute honesty, and a sense of vision that had been proven right many times, the organization followed his decisions, however unpopular. A trust had been built that the results would be worthy of the effort and direction.

A company does have to maintain a vision, long-term goals, and directives set forth by its leader. The vision tends to mold and guide all company decisions. For example, we want, simply, to do business in every part of the world. If it is feasible, we will continue to enter new nations, one or two a year. We are now operating in the People's Republic of China, India, Egypt, and Turkey. This colors the very way we think.

I ran into a friend a few years ago in Kennedy Airport in New York. He's the head of a large, east coast, chemical firm, and was just coming back from St. Martin. He asked where I was going.

"To inaugurate our new joint venture Egyptian plant," I said.

"Really," he said. "What are you doing there? I don't know anyone

This painting of the founder hangs in the Samuel Curtis Johnson Graduate School of Management at Cornell University.

else who is in Egypt."

Yet that is my very point. We are pioneering our business in different parts of the world. We are a leader. And the head of such an organization must be in the very forefront of the action.

This does, of course, mean taking risks. Taking the risks and the responsibility if they should fail. An organizational leader can't be totally involved with every project, but one does have to be part of it, helping the employees to win and bearing the risks of being wrong.

I have been wrong in my career plenty of times. I've been right more times, but I believe I've learned to accept making a mistake in a dignified way. If you're not willing to be wrong or to make a mistake, then you can't lead. Avoid the risks and you become a shepherd, not a leader.

There's nothing wrong with being a shepherd, keeping the flock from escaping and the wolves from the field. It is being protective, and there are people who have varying degrees of shepherding in their successful leadership styles. Yet it is different from being out front and leading.

Another prime element in leadership is in setting an example by how you work. You can't dabble in leadership; meeting with employees once a year, issuing orders from above the rest of the time are not enough. Leadership is an all-consuming occupation.

It should, moreover, extend outside the corporation. A leader must have a social conscience, an interest in the surrounding community, both within and outside of the company. It was Robert Louis Stevenson who wrote: "Perpetual devotion to what a man calls his business is only to be sustained by perpetual neglect of many other things." Well, one should not neglect the other things. And yet attention to the outside world will indeed reflect back down on the organization. A business leader who cares about schools in a town and holds loftier goals than the bottom line attracts an important amount of loyalty.

I believe that most people would rather be associated with a leader who has a social conscience, than with a man who says that the business of business is business. The notion that the bottom line is the only thing, that "What's good for General Motors is good for America," is passe. In recent years, it seems enterprise has been put into a much more proper role. And I hope that young people today recognize that business and business leadership are of a higher moral order than they were twenty-five or fifty years ago.

Recently I was given a copy of a book written some time back, called *John D.* It was an analysis of the life of John D. Rockefeller. This man was truly a leader, a man of religion and an individual with philanthropic inclinations. But he was painted in the book as ruthlessly competitive, a man who wasn't happy unless he had stamped out or acquired the business of a little guy. Actually, Rockefeller embodied all these qualities.

This is an interesting mix: Rockefeller resorted to trickery, false statements, and took competition to an extreme. He was also quite generous in giving away some of his money. But the former overshadowed the latter, and the John D.'s are not good enough for today's business and social climate.

One can and should be competitive. But sheer size is perhaps not the best measure of success. We have never said we wanted to be the biggest. We strive for something else that was once expressed well by Jim Allen of Booz, Allen and Hamilton. Jim told me: "I don't want to be the *biggest.* I just want to be the *best* consulting firm in the world." That was his vision for his company, and it is nearly identical to ours.

The pursuit of excellence is central. And it's a quality, or goal, that a leader should project. Mediocrity breeds mediocrity, while excellence breeds success. This extends from the way you keep your physical office to the way you treat people. Excellence should be reflected in every element of your business, right down to the way products are packaged.

Leaders, however, simply cannot take all the credit for success. In fact, a good leader tries to make heroes out of others. Most great leaders have monumental egos, so passing off credit isn't always the easiest thing to do. Yet it's crucial in building morale.

Building and recognizing heroes eventually bode well for the leader. If he doesn't worry about who gets the credit, or better, if he or she places the credit on an employee who did an excellent job, then in the long run the leader shares in the glory. Moreover, this stimulates creativity within the organization, for employees know they will be rewarded and recognized for their efforts.

As General Patton once wrote: "Never tell people *how* to do things. Tell them *what* to do and they will surprise you with their ingenuity." Then, when that ingenuity produces noteworthy results, ensure that the person who is responsible knows he is appreciated. This starts with the leader, and if the proper tone is set, every supervisor down the line will try to make the people working for him heroes. Finally, as the idea and behavior snowball, you have the man driving the forklift truck knowing that his boss cares, that his boss wants him to look good. And this is what keeps unions, a sure sign of dissatisfaction within a company, out.

James L. Allen, left, served for nineteen years on the Board of Directors and was personal counselor to Sam Johnson, at right. The occasion pictured was the dedication of the James L. Allen Center at Northwestern University.

"THIS IS THE BOSS' SON, SAM. HE'S GOING TO START AT THE BOTTOM FOR A FEW DAYS"

In the 1960s I was placed in a situation where I was in a room with Sam Rizzo, a United Auto Workers' leader. I told Sam I rarely had the chance to rub elbows with union people. In the course of our conversation, he said he never had the opportunity to organize our company. When I asked him what he meant, he replied: "Your company does two things that most companies don't," he explained. "You treat your people right—that is, you pay them well and deal with them right. But you also listen to them. And if you keep doing those two things, you will never have a union. But if you make a mistake on either, I'll *get* you!"

Listening and communicating. Again I come back to those qualities of leadership. They are so important that we have established three lines of communication for all our employees: the supervisory line, the personnel department line, and the line that goes around everybody else and leads directly to Sam.

That's right. Anyone who doesn't get a satisfactory answer from his supervisor can go up the line, with no fear of reprisals. And the process can lead all the way to my desk. It rarely happens, maybe only once or twice in the last several years. Perhaps it's because supervisors know they have to be responsive, or the employee will bring a problem to me. Maybe the knowledge that this final appeal process exists, ending at the leader's desk, is enough. I like to think it is part of an environment of open communication, a tone set by effective leadership, and a climate in which individuals, and an organization, can thrive.

PROFIT SHARING—FOR OUR COMMON CAUSE

". . . I truly believe we are a high-performing company because of profit sharing. Our earnings are better because of it."

Upon graduation from Harvard Business School, I naturally emerged full of opinions and ideas. And when I took a look at the company's profit sharing program, I figured that like a lot of other things at Johnson Wax, it was just another of my grandfather's archaic concepts. After all, *Harvard* offered no courses on profit sharing, and the management consultants of the country had not embraced it as a worthy idea.

Moreover, not only didn't Harvard have a formal profit sharing course, it wasn't even mentioned in other classes I'd taken. The fact that none of the university business schools ever picked up on profit sharing as a potentially major management tool was a near constant source of irritation for my father. Nonetheless, despite his feelings, how good could it be? Venerable Harvard, among others, gave the notion of profit sharing no credence.

Well, as I began to work at the company and came to understand what profit sharing was all about, I moved from being a cynic about the practice to being a believer totally committed to profit sharing. Although this transformation took a few years, I now believe that profit sharing, if properly managed, is one of the best means of drawing the entire company together into a common effort.

There are today a hard core of companies that continue to have profit sharing as a mainstream part of their corporation. And it's interesting that some of the major unions and the major companies for which they work are beginning to use the idea. Some politicians are beginning to see the role that profit sharing can play in making America more competitive. While profit sharing hasn't as yet caught fire across American industry, it's a concept that continues to have great potential for growth.

My father was one of the seven members of the organizing committee of the Profit Sharing Council of America, a group that had twenty-two charter members, including Johnson Wax. Until very recently, when there was a severe slowdown in American business, the number of members in the Council was growing, but membership has stalled. The past growth trend that the Council experienced was a good sign, and it is hoped that the trend will resume now that the Council has made growth a major objective. Profit sharing has worked so well for us, just as it has for other companies where the concept has been set up properly and managed right. Basically, it has to be established in a corporation where there is a mutual confidence and trust between hourly people, salaried people, and management. Profit sharing doesn't usually work well in unionized firms, although there are now more union companies where it does thrive. But that's only where there are good union-management relationships and feelings of mutual confidence.

Simply handing out a percentage of the profits once a year is not, however, enough to make such a plan work. For profit sharing to succeed, you've got to have a number of other elements working in conjunction:

• To begin with, you've got to encourage upwards communication, at all levels, from the hourly people to the management. And just as important is downward communication, a clear articulation by management of its goals and what it expects of the people.

• The amount of money has to be meaningful to the employees. A turkey at Christmas time will not suffice. It's got to be significant, and in our case that means twenty-five percent of corporate profits before taxes, after setting aside a reasonable return for shareholders. That twenty-five percent is important, in that it can mean up to two months' pay to someone in the factory.

• Profit sharing also extends from the executive suite to the factory, for if it's going to work it has to be universal. If only the executives can share in the riches, then what you've got is just a bonus program. It's therefore not true profit sharing, unless all contributors to the success of the company share in it to a certain degree.

• The program cannot, I should stress, be a substitute for fair wages. It's an add-on to fair pay. If you try to make it a substitute for equitable wages, then the profit sharing plan is bound for disaster. If you use profit sharing to make up a deficit in your pay plans—in an effort to correct what's essentially a mistake—you have violated the basic concept of the plan. A company that attempts this also violates the spirit of the concept, with results that surely will not bode well for anyone in the company.

• Profit sharing has to be consistent. That is, you don't arbitrarily change the formula every year, or else your people will lose confidence in the program and faith in the company's management. The amount of money has to go up when profits go up, and go down when the profits fall. Should a firm try to smooth out the bumps by paying less during a good year, or paying more during a bad one, then it becomes meaningless. There is then no true sense of sharing in the successes and failures of the company as you go through the years.

Therefore, we've had essentially the same formula since our profit sharing began in 1917. In that first year, 193 employees shared $31,250. Today, tens of millions of dollars in profit shares are distributed to Johnson employees each year. We have had to adapt to certain new conditions, such as changes in the capital structure of the company, acquisitions, and the addition of new companies outside the U.S.

One recent change was related to the growing international character of the company. Few multinational corporations share their profits with employees in other countries. Among those that do, a common practice is to base the profit sharing on worldwide earnings, such as is done at Texas Instruments. We base profit sharing plans on locally earned profits.

In the past, when we calculated the U.S. profit sharing pool, we included all the expenses for providing services to our international subsidiaries. During the years when we had subsidiaries in only France and England, and my father made only a few trips there each year, it didn't matter much. But today our Racine employees provide these far-flung and large foreign operations with a tremendous amount of support. We wanted to give credit to them for their part of international sales.

Indeed, about sixty percent of our business—and more than two-thirds of our employee workforce—lies outside the United States. But Racine personnel provide research and development services, management, and computer services for these worldwide groups. We therefore made adjustments so that the Racine people would get profit sharing on the profits generated in the United States, and also would be credited for all the effort put into the support of our large, overseas group of companies.

Such adjustments are designed to keep equity in the plan and ensure its fairness. But changes don't happen very often, and we never arbitrarily shift the formula up or down.

The philosophical underpinnings of our profit sharing plan stem from my grandfather, who had a genuine sense of wanting to share the success of the enterprise with those who made it possible. Recall that in 1917 most people thought "involvement" and "concern" were just words with little relevance to the worlds of industry and commerce. Businessmen rarely gave away anything they weren't forced to relinquish. Yet my grandfather applied creative imagination

The first Profit Sharing Day get-together at Christmas 1917 was held in a factory warehouse. Profit sharing continues to be a cornerstone of company policy.

to personnel relations. It worked well with 150 to 200 employees. Although communications can grow complicated, there's no reason it can't work for 11,500 people, our size today. But preserving the sense of family is not easy, and getting across the concept that everybody is on the same side of the table and faces the same set of objectives that will help the firm succeed gets a little more difficult.

I think the reason profit sharing hasn't become more popular in large companies is that most big firms have a more confrontational relationship between management and labor. It's hard to establish profit sharing when the people on the production line say, "Just give us more pay." Or, "I want to know what I'm going to get next year. I don't want to depend on how well you big shots do in managing the company."

Profit sharing is not simply a way to keep contentious unions out of a company. It's not even a compensation program. No, it's something totally apart, and actually is quite consistent with some of the new concepts of management we're learning from the Japanese, in particular, the idea of participatory management.

This starts with "quality circles" on the shop floor, with responsibility for quality vested as much in the person on the line as in the supervisor, and with a management responsive to idea generation. Profit sharing supports these so-called new methods of management. But I suspect that by virtue of our profit sharing, the kind of atmosphere that engenders such "Japanese-style" cooperation has been around Johnson Wax for a long time. Profit sharing breeds and nurtures that sense of participation, that attention to quality. Not surprisingly, we had little trouble instituting profit sharing in our Japanese operations. It fit their psychology and management style perfectly.

Does profit sharing, however, really make the average employee more satisfied? I think it does, so long as they are paid fairly and get the profit sharing on top of it. When an employee receives a letter from the President that says we've had a good year, that sales and profit sharing are much better than last year, and that here's your first half payment on what we've achieved, then the employee has to feel he's part of the process. He must think, "I helped the company earn that money. I helped that surplus called profits to happen." Consequently, all Johnson employees are acutely aware that profit sharing is absolutely dependent on profit making!

This awareness is a dynamic force in a company. But it is something that needs the constant reinforcement which comes from communication. We don't always do as good a job of communicating as we can, but we certainly try. We still have the annual Christmas party. Sure, every company has one, but unless our people attend, they don't get their profit sharing checks on time. Just being there rubbing elbows with everyone is a thrill. One probably has to be there to understand the emotions of the experience; we sometimes take the practice for granted, but it has served the company well.

There have been times when we've felt compelled to redouble our communications efforts. For example, we expanded the *Johnson Weekly* to include more profit sharing news. We revitalized the publication not long ago, and also created a productivity awareness. Productivity is something that can be closely related to profit sharing. We made productivity improvements in the factory, and it's something that is reflected in the profit sharing checks.

I've often been amazed at how well profit sharing has worked overseas, especially in developing nations. It is a very fundamental and basic free enterprise concept, one that makes every employee a solid capitalist. When you measure the success of profit sharing—and by analogy, capitalism—against the communist ideology that is so often espoused in the Third World, the results are quite startling.

As a means of improving the lot of Third World nations, communism has been an incredible failure. Communist leaders can't easily back away from the system, for it is their way of holding onto power. Communism has taken individual incentive out of the entire institutional workplace. The only incentive is to become a bigger bureaucrat, and bureaucracies add little to a society. Moreover, when all the fruits of labor belong to the state, well, it just doesn't drive employees to grow more fruit. However, if some of those fruits come back to the employee through profit sharing, then you have strong, built-in incentives for employees.

Profit sharing is, of course, at odds with classic capitalism. Milton Friedman's intellectual description of capitalism is that management must always maximize the bottom line, which will ultimately raise the lot of everyone. Some might say that profit sharing cuts into that bottom line. Still, I think it's a worthy "sacrifice." Or, better said, a worthy modification, for I truly believe we are a high-performing company because of profit sharing. Our earnings are better because of it.

For this reason I'd stand behind profit sharing even if Johnson Wax were a public company. Because the practice creates a better sense of participation and sharing, is in the employees' and the institution's interest, and does markedly affect long-term profits for the better, I would never apologize to shareholders about sharing the profits with all our people.

Every time a bad product goes off the end of the line, it hurts the company's reputation and eventually its earnings. But if there's an individual there—in the research lab or in the factory—who makes the instant connection between the quality of products, the company's reputation, its impact on earnings, and how that reaches into his profit sharing check, then he's going to do something to keep that bad product from going out. And this is a special advantage not many companies have.

Look at the corporations that are in trouble in the United States, the companies in basic industries that are coming unglued, such as in steel, automotive, and capital equipment. Granted, they have complex problems, starting with some old and inefficient plants and with the competition posed by lower wages overseas. Many modern Pacific Rim factories are doing better than America's. But not all of them are that much more efficient. Therefore, I begin to suspect that something else is missing in some of these U.S. corporations.

When the four-millionth Spring Glo-Coat deal (eight million cans) came off the Johnson filling line on March 31, 1947, it marked a major milestone in production and made a major contribution to profit sharing that year.

I wonder if the missing elements are in the management system or in the spirit in which employees are compensated for their labor. Perhaps the aura of contention that has grown between management and labor is indelible in many of these corporations and industries. Perhaps many in our society are incapable of functioning in a "quality circle," as do workers in Japan. The Western culture is one of individualism, shaded with a touch of selfishness. Given this, it is tough to expect a worker to expend his all for a company when he can't be sure of commensurate rewards for his effort.

Over the years one of the basic complaints of workers is that they have no say in how they do their work, that the mechanics of the job are dictated by management, leaving no room for individual initiative and creativity. Savvy corporations have recognized the error of this and have brought employees into participatory management circles, accepting the good suggestions and allowing everyone to become part of the work process. So there is some hope.

Communication. Again and again the need for management to reach the workforce is apparent. From experience we've found that to gain maximum benefit from the profit sharing plan—for employees and the corporation—there must be a clear understanding on the part of all involved of the goals of the company, its policies, and preparations for the future. We've learned that it is necessary to tell and retell the philosophy behind all our programs, regardless of how successful they've been in the past. And profit sharing establishes perhaps our best line of communication.

Back in 1947 my father said, "The fundamental reason for starting profit sharing at our business was to find some additional means of making Johnson people aware of their importance to the business, aware of participating in the success of the organization as well as the work. The employee has to be aware that he or she is a part of the company, rather than just a hired hand at so much an hour, week or month; aware that he or she is an individual playing on the team."

This statement is a good synopsis of literally dozens of business tomes you can find in bookstores today: books that tout the Japanese way of managing a corporation or point out the productive atmosphere of a few excellent American companies. For nearly seven decades, this sentiment has been a guiding force at Johnson Wax. Curiously, the notion is as fresh, invigorating, and useful now as when Woodrow Wilson sat in the White House.

WISE COUNSEL—THE NEED FOR OUTSIDE ADVICE

"Credible advisors will disagree with you and say things you really don't want to hear . . . but should."

More family enterprises have gone astray through a lack of good advice than for any other single reason. Understand that the head of a family business receives plenty of suggestions; but as Ambrose Bierce pointed out in *The Devil's Dictionary*, advice can be defined as "the smallest current coin." What we're talking about is good, solid, and objective consultations.

All corporations, private and public, large or small, occasionally (if not constantly) need the counsel of experts who come from outside the management structure. Such individuals can be "outside" members on the board of directors or consultants specializing in a specific element of, for instance, manufacturing. They can bring with them a special perspective that is not always found in a full-time executive or employee, however talented. An advisor who is, if you will, undomesticated, can often make the hard recommendations from which staffers may quite naturally retreat.

The need for sound outside advice is particularly acute in a family business. Much of this is due to the intrinsic characteristics of most family enterprises. Here you have "Dad," the company's founder, answering only to "Mom," Uncle Charlie, and Aunt Millie—the shareholders in the business. And later, of course, there are Dad's children and nieces and nephews, all of whom have a stake in the operation.

The founder of the company is usually struggling to get something going, building a new business, and doing it on his own wits. He certainly cannot afford consultants; he can barely afford an accountant, and in many cases doesn't even have one. All he knows is that he has a better mousetrap and is destined to make a million dollars with it. Or, he's found a gold mine and is going to exploit it. He sure as heck is not going to hire a mining consultant, because he's going to keep the location of the mine a secret. The same thing applies to the better mousetrap: no one outside the family is going to see the device until it hits the market.

That same syndrome exists even in larger and well-established family companies, where there is a sense of privacy and a conviction that you know how to do it yourself. Moreover, there may be plenty of input from other members of the family, who at least think they know quite a bit about the operation. Consequently, the founder/ entrepreneur can be put in the position of having to defend himself from others in the family.

Most entrepreneurs running family companies have never had a formal business school education. Even if they had, they would have found that schools rarely teach the value of properly using a consulting firm. Business schools hardly impart the awful truth that lawyers are necessary in one's corporate life, even though their background moves them to look at problems and opportunities in a negative way. Anyway, future planning is something that usually isn't in the mind of the entrepreneur, because basically he's just surviving, managing the quest as a day-to-day fight.

However, planning and getting good advice from outside the company are, simply, critical. This became apparent to my father when his career started in 1928, upon the death of his father. My grandfather passed away without leaving a will, and it took my father, who was then twenty-eight years old, about eleven years to sort out the details of the business. He decided at that time that no other member of the family would ever have to go through such problems again. He started doing his planning.

My father, moreover, realized that he wasn't the smartest person concerning every part of the business. He had the wisdom, I think, to recognize that perhaps the duty of the head of a business was to gather around him people who were smarter than he was in certain areas. To be successful as the head of an enterprise, you don't necessarily have to be the brightest in all aspects of the operation, but you have to be certain you get the best available advice.

Ultimately this is just as good as having the knowledge yourself. For example, when my father wanted advice on how to build an office building, he turned to Frank Lloyd Wright, who you could say was a consultant in architecture. The structure we got was the product of the interaction between my father and Wright.

Very early in his business career my father developed the idea that you need objective and creative help in making decisions. In addition, in a family enterprise, you need a defense—a backup opinion supporting your position—against someone like Uncle Charlie, who believes he is a wizard on all matters. When Charlie thinks he has a notion that will sweep the marketing department to record performance, one needs a marketing consultant to verify (but more likely destroy) the proposal. If Charlie has an advertising campaign idea in hand, the company should retain a trusted and professional advertising consultant. But no matter the Uncle Charlies of the world; just having a general management consultant can help a company in many, many ways.

Fortunately, my father had his brother-in-law, Jack Louis, at his side to help in the early days of radio advertising. He and his associates at Needham, Louis and Brorby created "Fibber McGee and Molly," which became the most popular radio program for many years. Uncle Jack's wise and friendly advice in media advertising helped launch our company as a major consumer products company. So, in some instances, a family team is very important.

While in the initial stages of developing the business, my father got Edwin G. Booz to join our board of directors. Booz was one of the founders of the noted consulting firm of Booz, Allen and Hamilton,

H. F. Johnson (left) had his brother-in-law Jack Louis to advise him on media advertising. Louis brought the "Fibber McGee & Molly Show" to Johnson Wax.

Edwin G. Booz, one of the founders of Booz Allen Management Consultants, was among the early counselors employed by H. F. Johnson.

and he helped my father make many crucial decisions about Johnson Wax. Later, my father persuaded James Allen of the same firm to follow Ed Booz on the Johnson board. What these men did, above all, was to help my father clearly express his leadership. Simply put, his leadership carried more impact because not only was he stating his own opinions, but on major matters he was presenting the opinions of what was then, and still is, one of the largest and most reputable consulting firms in the country.

As a result of this particular directorship—first Booz and then Allen—my father decided that if one outside director was a good idea, then having a majority of outside directors might be an even better idea. Then, my father would not have to vote against the family or the management on any question, for the majority of independent views would carry the day. These were very intelligent and independent people, and of course they wouldn't always agree with my father. On the other hand, unlike family- or management-dominated boards they certainly would not gang up on him for any special interest that they might have had.

A board composed mostly of outside individuals, strong and reputable professionals, can act in the best interest of the company. And that is what you need in a family business: decisions that ensure the future of the enterprise, which are not clouded by the short-term considerations, or perhaps selfish interests, of family members or managers who may think more in terms of themselves than the company.

Because of the natural tendency for a family business to become inbred—to nurture a "know-it-all" attitude—we developed the ideas of having independent directors and using independent consultants liberally in many different fields. These include design consultants, estate planning consultants, experts on public relations, tax planners, whatever. My father believed in getting the best of outside advice to augment our internal talent, and that is something we continue to do. I'm convinced that one of the reasons for the success of the company was that we were able to attract and hold some of the top outside advisors in the country.

Such counsel can do more than help a CEO. Indeed, consultants can be invaluable to inside managers, especially when they are about to go up against the man who owns the company. The consultant can make the recommendation. If he gets shot down, fine; he gets shot down. But the employee doesn't end up in flames.

This eases the flow of upward communication to management. For example, if somebody from manufacturing comes in and recommends we build a high-speed conveyor line that will greatly help our manufacturing effort, but will cost twenty million dollars, well, it's going to put a few lumps in some throats. But if he backs the proposal with an analysis from one of the top engineering consultants in the business, who points out that the line will be among the best in the world and will give the company a competitive edge, then the idea has double endorsement.

In a private company there can often be, however, a reluctance to use consulting help. For one thing, consultants can violate the company's sense of privacy, and for another they can run up against the all-too-common resistance to ideas "not invented here." You can, to be sure, overuse consultants, for example, turning to one when you have exceptional internal capabilities, or when the problem is of low risk.

I have to admit that there have been times when we may have been "over-consulted," almost having consultants who consult with consultants. That gets a bit ridiculous, especially as we get bigger and more diversified, with an in-house staff loaded with expertise. Advice from our own people in many cases can be much better than what consultants can bring to us. One should use outside resources well, but wisely.

One of the key roles for an independent director or consultant in a family business is helping overcome the generational gap which can occur between the head of the company and one or more of his children, who are coming up behind, feeling their oats, and itching to take things into their own hands. The younger generation (this was as true fifty years ago as it is today) has a spirit that compels them to want to do things differently. They have well-meaning differences with father, the CEO, and the young people simply want to make their unique mark. And yet this can cause serious family rifts.

Sadly, perhaps, there are many instances of children of entrepreneurs of very successful companies who choose not to go into the family business. While the progeny might well do wonderful things in the family company, they are put off when attempts to resolve differences with the "old man" do not go well. In turn, they decide to make their own mark outside the company, rather than sitting around having arguments with their father about which direction the company ought to go. In many cases there is a genuine desire on their parts to have careers of their own without any help from the family or company.

This is where the independent counselor comes in and has a valuable role to play. In my case there were two individuals between me and my father: James Allen, since the beginning of my career, and then later, Harold Stassen. Both played a tremendous part in

As an expression of appreciation for his services as a special counsel to the corporation and the family, Harold E. Stassen earned a commendation, presented to him at the company's Centennial Dinner, held in Washington, D.C. in June 1986. With him when he accepted the honor was his wife Esther.

buffering potential problems.

I could tell Jim Allen what was bothering me; I could be straight, strong, and use terms that would have gotten me tossed headfirst out of my father's office. Allen would just soak it in, and never get mad. He would say, "Well, Sam, I agree with you on this, but I don't agree with you on that." I never got mad at him for telling me I was wrong about something, for there was none of that tension that routinely exists between a father and son. Moreover, I could trust Jim Allen because he was a consultant with a superb reputation, and I knew how he would deal discreetly with my father.

You see, he could lay out my opinion to my father, who might well say, "Sam is way off beam on this. Crazy, in fact. What's that boy thinking?" Should I hear that reaction, our working relationship would sink faster than the *Titanic*. But Allen could filter the two viewpoints, create a solution, and put us onto a mutually agreeable track, without anyone getting angry.

Time and again Jim Allen would come back to me and calmly explain things. "You know, Sam, maybe your idea ought to move slightly in this direction. And if you did it, I think your father just might go along with it and be satisfied." And then Allen would offer to go back to my father with "my" compromise proposal. Of course, I knew he had worked on it with my father in advance and that Jim would take back only something which he would most likely approve. But the system worked and was a way of buffering almost inevitable confrontations.

There were clashes. And there also were heartwarming moments when my father would look me in the eye and say, "That was a good job, Sam." It didn't happen very often, but it nonetheless happened. But, if my father were upset with me, he didn't have to approach me directly. He could go through the channels of a consultant or outside director. We did talk directly at times, particularly after he became ill. But more often were the occasions when Harold Stassen would talk to my father, talk to me, go back to him, and then return to me.

If I tried to tell my father that he was too ill to attend a meeting, he would surely go into a rage. "What are you trying to do," he'd storm, "trying to keep me out of everything?" But Stassen could say to him, "You're an old friend of mine. I'm even older than you are. You shouldn't go to that meeting because it isn't good for your health. Sam is perfectly capable and you have good people who can handle it. Do me a favor and don't go." Then my father wouldn't go. Having someone like Stassen make such a suggestion didn't spur the instinctive resistance that would occur had I done it.

High level officers of the company can also serve the same purpose. Bringing our son Curt into the business as a venture capitalist is a classic example of using intermediaries. I requested several key officers and consultants to study the concept, after Curt had determined that this was the only way that he would enter the firm. Together they worked up the entire venture capital structure. This was a whole new business for the company, and an example of the next generation's bringing something entirely new to the enterprise.

A private committee of independent directors—four in all— endorsed the plan. Since these directors agreed that it was a good business idea, it couldn't be attacked for being an inside job backed strictly by one of the company's "family" members. And as Curt carried the proposal to fruition, he felt comfortable that he had sold the company on it, and not just his old man. Some very important business people had first been convinced of its wisdom. So, I just don't see how anyone can operate a family business without consultation with people to act as buffers, who can keep lines of communication and understanding open among the family, the management, and the next generation.

There is always going to be some infighting in a family enterprise. While it doesn't have to be as bad as on the TV show "Dallas," there are jealousies within families. Siblings have a natural competitiveness;

fathers, mothers, and offspring have differences.

I like to tell the story about an entrepreneur who was watching his son begin to take over the business he created. But when he thinks about it for a while, he says, "You know that young squirt is fooling around with my mistress, that's what he is doing." The company was the man's mistress, for he was in love with his business. He has to get over an emotional high hurdle when he sees his son messing around with what, next to his wife, he may love more than anything else. A business organization can be like a baby, wife, and mistress wrapped into a single entity. It can be your reason for being in this world, whether you built it from scratch or simply run it. Dealing with a brash kid who wants control—and having no help from intermediaries—can create an interpersonal minefield.

One does make mistakes on the way up, and one's growth in running a company is as much a maturing process as a learning process. The maturing comes with the development of self-confidence. And the more self-confidence you develop, the more you are willing to seek outside advice, because you recognize that it is not a sign of weakness.

Asking an expert for help increases your odds of success. You not

The U.S. and Canadian Johnson Boards held a joint meeting in Washington, D.C. in 1986 in conjunction with the premiere at the National Air and Space Museum of "On the Wing."

Seated, from left, Richard M. Thomson (C), John J. Louis Jr. (U.S.), Samuel C. Johnson, J. Paul Sticht (U.S.) and John J. Wettlaufer (C).

Standing, from left Raymond F. Farley (U.S.), George W. Delp (C), Frank F. Wiley (C), John A. Pollock (C), Mary Alice Stuart (C), Lester E. Coleman (U.S.), Fred B. Dent (U.S.) and William P. Stiritz (U.S.).

only need the humility to admit mistakes, but also the ability to learn and mature with the assistance of others. I have notions of my own, but what I really want to do before making a decision is to reap all I can get from the brains of others. When sitting around the table with advisors, I'll try to get everyone there to nod their heads—in genuine consensus. On the other hand, I will go my own way if I think I've got a better solution, sometimes based on instincts alone.

The ability to get the best advice is an important quality of leadership. But in the words of Publilius Syrus, from about the first century B.C., "Many receive advice, only the wise profit from it." The thing is, you have to know when and how to use it.

I believe that if Richard Nixon had not gotten himself so wrapped up with those advisors in his inner circle, he would have had little problem with Watergate. Those counselors "yes-manned" him right out of the White House. If he had said, the day after the Watergate break-in, "Yes, I heard about it from my people, it shouldn't have happened and they will be disciplined," then he might have been OK. As the President said on "Meet The Press" on April 10, 1988, "We fouled it up beyond belief. It was a great mistake. It was wrong—and apart from the fact it was wrong, it was stupid." He said he should have dealt with it and dealt with it fast. He had dragged his feet while listening to his few confidants. Had he been open to a little wider range of advice, he'd have been aware of the dangers of stonewalling and never would have pushed himself into a trap.

Credible advisors will disagree with you and say things you really don't want to hear. This is the way it should be. We have really credible, independent people on our board today. Sometimes they disagree with me, other board members, or the management. The disagreements are always constructive and meant to move the company forward. Many times I feel them out in advance to avoid confrontation at the meeting. A board must move as a group, and it takes an element of leadership to develop a climate where it can come up with joint decisions with which everyone on the board is reasonably happy. Having multiple camps on the board of directors and family internal politics intruding into the business are just not healthy conditions.

Of course, consultants are not your meat and potatoes. You have to expect objectivity from your own executives, too. And some of them sometimes develop the habit of telling you what they think you want to hear. (They don't last long.) Therefore, you have to make it clear to both outside advisors and your internal management that you want the information and opinions straight. Make it clear, moreover, that you're not a "shoot the messenger" type.

It helps, I believe, to have a consulting firm (or one person from that firm) do more than one job over a period of years. That way they get to know the company, its culture, practices, and approaches to business problems. Take Chuck Allison of Booz, Allen and Hamilton, who has been working with me for more than twenty years. He knows me, my strengths and weaknesses. He knows Johnson Wax, our basic strategy, and how the company treats its people. Allison is never going to come up with an outlandish recommendation that might be perfect for General Motors, but would never work here. So there is value to continuity in consultants. They have a familiarity, tempered by the necessary distance, and diversity of experience, to give objective help.

An Uncle Charlie is never going to be entirely objective. And in a family enterprise he's going to make his voice heard. Moreover, he's usually going to offer his opinion that his nephew, the CEO, is a born dummy. Having top notch directors and consultants, with reputations that even Charlie has to respect, is going to keep order, if not peace, in the family business. And on the whole, the company is going to be better for all the well-considered outside assistance.

DIVERSIFICATION

". . . without new products a business almost invariably stagnates."

The S. C. Johnson Company started in business as a manufacturer of parquet flooring. Whenever my great-grandfather and grandfather learned of a new house being constructed, they would quickly strike a deal with the owner for the home's flooring. Then they took the parquet pieces that had been cut in the company's small factory, loaded them onto a horse-drawn wagon, and hauled them to the building site. Carpenters did the installation.

That, essentially, was the company's business. And parquet flooring remained the firm's main endeavor when it became the S. C. Johnson & Son partnership in 1906. Moreover, had the enterprise stayed in the parquetry business, it is conceivable that we might still be making wood floors.

I'd like to believe we would be a downright excellent wood floormaker, supplying our product to new and remodeled homes in our area, probably throughout the Midwest, and perhaps even nationally. The company no doubt would have grown over the decades, but as synthetic flooring—such as linoleum, rubber, and vinyl tile—became more popular, we surely would have found ourselves scrambling to compete in a declining market. I suspect that if S. C. Johnson had stayed exclusively with parquet flooring, the company would have generated perhaps $20 to $30 million a year in business, employing several hundred people in Racine. We also would have been caught, twisted, and torn over the years by the ups and downs of the home construction industry.

However, my great-grandfather made a crucial decision, although I don't think he believed it was so crucial at the time. He began supplying his customers with the finishes used on wood floors: the sealers, varnishes, and shellacs that looked good, but were difficult to apply, maintain, and remove. When he developed Johnson's Prepared Wax™—a combination of naphtha, beeswax, paraffin, and some harder waxes—he probably thought he was merely providing an additional service.

What he had really done was to take a first step towards diversification, something that is now a fundamental part of our corporate strategy and culture. My great-grandfather also should be given credit for recognizing the potential of diversification, for he could have simply stayed with the parquet and sold a little wax on the side. Instead, he had the foresight to develop the wax business, and what he started is continuing today.

We frequently introduce new brands and new products into new markets. They are signs of the company's growth and regeneration, for without new products a business almost invariably stagnates. My great-grandfather did not necessarily understand this. Nor at that point was it crucial for him to think about such a strategy. But when he discovered that some people who had not purchased his floors were nevertheless buying his wax and using it on floors made and installed by other companies, he realized he might have stumbled onto a significant addition to his business.

As my great-grandfather's reputation as a wax maker spread, he had the wherewithal to help it along by taking out advertising. Moreover, he knew the hardware business—having once been in it— and began calling on store owners. He knew these businessmen would

The original business was parquet flooring, and here, the production crew assembled before examples of their wares. It was when S. C. Johnson enclosed samples of Prepared Wax with each shipment of flooring that the company came to be known as wood finishing authorities.

prefer selling several dozen cans of 29-cent wax rather than waiting for a homebuilder to buy a living room floor.

Once the idea that the wax market might be bigger than the market for floors crystallized in my great-grandfather's mind, he began to concentrate on selling his new product in a wider geographic area. He was a believer in advertising, and when he had enough money he promoted Johnson's Prepared Wax™ in *The Saturday Evening Post* and other prestigious, general circulation magazines. It wasn't long before Johnson's was a national brand.

The diversification from parquet flooring into floor wax had an impact far more profound than adding to the company's sales. Indeed, it stimulated a whole new way of thinking within the firm. And the basic line of thought came down to this question: If the wax worked so well on floors, what about on other surfaces?

In 1898, right in tune with the Gay Nineties, the company introduced Dance Wax,™ a powdered product to be sprinkled on a floor before dances. It allowed revelers to glide over the floor with much more grace than otherwise would have been possible. Then, in 1914, when Henry Ford's six-year-old Model-T was really beginning to catch fire with consumers—and about 1,000 cars per day were being produced—my grandfather brought out Johnson's Auto Wax and Cleaner.™ This opened a whole new market, although using the same kind of product the company made for floors.

By 1917 the style of home decor had changed and parquet flooring had dropped in popularity. Had S. C. Johnson & Son not also been in the wax business, it would have suffered mightily. But in that year the company made its last shipment of flooring; diversification had actually taken the firm into a new era.

The company's automobile products were flourishing. The line was expanded to include a number of Johnson "Car Savers," such as Stop Squeak Oil, Self-Vulcanizer, Radiator Cement, and Hastee Patch, all fine products for the time. Other introductions did not fare as well, like the infamous Freeze Proof, intended for the radiator of a Model-T. Not long after bringing out the product, the company learned that Freeze Proof dissolved Model-T radiators. In 1918, S. C. Johnson & Son acquired title to roughly 500 useless radiators.

It soon became obvious to my grandfather that having a chemist in the company's employ was an absolute requirement if he were to diversify still further. He needed someone to formulate new products properly. Curiously enough, he selected my father to fill the role. But first he had to send his young chemist away for schooling.

Dispatched to Cornell University to study the science, my father returned to the company in 1922. He was, in fact, the first graduate

Freeze Proof for radiators was a chemical experiment that convinced Mr. Herbert F. Johnson Sr. that the company needed trained chemists on staff.

The first diversification was to Johnson's Prepared Paste Wax. This is one of the early national ads which kept the spotlight on the flooring business, but gave emphasis to wax - Johnson's Wax.

chemist the business ever had. Moreover, my father never forgot his basic training in chemistry and its attendant impact on research and development. My father literally championed this end of the business, just as my grandfather had supported the concept of advertising.

Throughout the 1920s the company built upon existing products and branched into new areas. A carbon remover for auto engines was marketed, in addition to an electric floor polisher. The polisher was, of course, quite different from anything the company had sold before, but nonetheless it related to our basic wax business. In 1928 the company even had a wax for airplanes!

Johnson Wax was in the floor polisher business from the start. Electric floor polishers came into the picture in 1925. The streamlined model, standing before then Public Relations Vice President William N. Connolly, was introduced in 1957. Johnson Wax went out of the consumer floor polisher market in the early 1960s.

Some tests allegedly showed that wax reduced the frictional drag on aircraft three to ten percent, and so the company experimented. Later, Sam Johnson, a pilot and aviation buff, ran tests of his own and couldn't prove that wax made a bit of difference — though it made the plane look great!

My father bought an airplane so he could test the wax. It was called, appropriately enough, the "Johnson Waxbird." Tests conducted at the Guggenheim Foundation allegedly showed that the wax reduced the frictional drag upon the craft by three to ten percent. In my heart I believed the claims were doubtful, and years later I ran some tests of my own while I was in the Technical Services department. We waxed several American Airlines planes, and could never prove it made a bit of difference. Now perhaps on a fabric-skinned plane it may have helped, but on metal crafts the rivets catch the air whether waxed or not.

During the first years of the Great Depression the company's business dropped from $5 million per year to $3 million. However, this was the period when my father brought out Glo-Coat,™ a self-polishing floor wax that was a revolutionary product. Its success proved that a superior product can come to market and thrive, even during poor economic times.

The Golden Age of Radio was also a golden opportunity for Johnson Wax. Radio advertising, in particular the company's connection with the "Fibber McGee and Molly" show as previously mentioned, helped the business boom. And new products kept coming, mostly wax items, but formulated for new uses. There were waxes for large institutional buildings—a gymnasium finish, a cream wax, and a furniture polish. We developed waxes for about anything you could think of around the home, school, church, and hospital.

When World War II began, Johnson Wax diversified into products for the war effort, like rifle bore cleaner. The company was becoming practiced at new product development now, devising formulations for a laundry product called Drax and paints that included a wax called Wax-o-Namel. Our paint business never really got going, though. As with the radiator formula, the company's intentions were sound, but a crucial element was missing to make the paint successful. No, Wax-o-Namel didn't cause houses to dissolve, but we were eventually compelled to get out of the paint business because it didn't fit our distribution patterns. We had the technology, but found it difficult to compete with the Du Ponts, Sherwin Williams, and other large companies. Most of our products were targeted for grocery store sales, and paints are not.

Although we continued to diversify right through the first half of the 1950s, the majority of the company's products were in the floor care, furniture care, auto care, or surface care field. When I joined the firm in 1954, my father said that the only way we would increase sales volume was to come up with even more new products. So he had me organize the new products department.

It took about two years of trial and error, but when I convinced my father that Raid™ House and Garden Insecticide could be a winner, we made an important break from the wax business. Moreover, the idea was much like Johnson's Prepared Wax™—a seminal product off which others could grow. "Raid™ kills bugs dead," became our advertising slogan. Indeed, insecticides are our biggest single product group worldwide today.

It is important to note that our corporate health owes a great deal to these early and frequent diversification efforts. Companies that are extinct today, like the Schlitz Brewery, failed to recognize the need to spread risk. You see, Schlitz management believed that the beer business would continue growing in the same pattern that it had for years, that if you had one good brand, it was all you needed. Beer drinkers, however, began demanding a choice. They wanted light beers, dark beers, and foreign beers, and were willing to drink all three from the same brewer if they were only offered the option. Some brewers recognized this and were able to capitalize on the consumers' demands for choice. Michelob, for example, comes in light, dark, and regular; their marketing plan has been a successful form of diversification. Schlitz, on the other hand, made several grievous business mistakes, but I think failing to diversify successfully was a most damaging error.

It is also important that you recognize when you have a multiple-brand marketing opportunity in your hands—when you have what,

48

with a little imagination, is an entirely new product. For instance, our research and development people came up with an improvement in the Glo-Coat™ formula, the original self-polishing floor wax. The improvement was a milky-white product, which was not as heavy-duty as Glo-Coat,™ smelled different, and didn't tend to yellow a floor as much as the original. I was still the New Products director, and when our marketing director, Stuart Watson, told me, "Sam, this is not a new Glo-Coat,™ it's a new brand," I became convinced that he had a point, and that we had a new marketing opportunity.

My father was not as easily swayed, and at first he challenged me. "Why don't you just put the best product you know how to make in the Glo-Coat™ can?" he asked. I told him I wasn't sure that the new formula was better for all consumers. "But it's different," I explained. "And I think that some consumers might like it better than Glo-Coat,™ and others will stick with the older product. Either way, we can make some unique claims with the new formula." Eventually he came around, and we introduced a new floor wax, Klear,™ to the market.

Klear™ cannibalized some of Glo-Coat's market, but overall we picked up a ten-point share gain in the business. Putting out brands that compete with others you own is a form of diversification which also expands the market, with the sum of the two putting the company further ahead. I am continually amazed that more companies do not follow this course, and that they still believe that only one product will appeal to everyone. The automobile makers learned long ago about the value of choices. But some have learned that choice is not more important than quality.

A company also can diversify into markets that previously didn't exist, or were of less than noteworthy size. The brewers that came out with a light beer provide an example of what can be accomplished. And then there is our experience with the insect repellent Off!™ In 1956 or 1957, the entire United States market for insect repellents was less than $2 million, a very small business. It's no wonder: most of the anti-bug concoctions were made of citronella, bear grease, and other ingredients that didn't smell that great, and didn't work very well either.

However, when we got into the insecticide business, we began to tour companies that supplied chemicals. One of these, Hercules Chemicals, was a company that one of our chemists, making a routine literature search in U.S. Department of Agriculture materials, learned was making a chemical we know as deet. On our tour, one of their people approached us, put a bottle of clear material on the table, and said, "We developed this new insect repellent for the U.S. Army and it works better than anything we've ever seen. We are trying to sell it to the Army, but we don't have the marketing capacity for doing much else with it."

I took a sample of the formula back to our marketing people. Their reaction was negative, based on the plain fact that virtually no insect repellent was sold in food stores—our primary distribution network. But I thought this might be a market we could *create*, or at the very least build, simply because we had an excellent product in our hands. I thought of all those kids being attacked in their back yards each summer, and all the mothers who would love to prevent their children from getting bitten by mosquitoes. That need, and a good product, I reasoned, would equal a dynamic diversification.

We used advertising to educate the public on the use of insect repellent, since mothers, our target market, didn't frequent sporting goods stores (where the product previously was found), and they didn't know insect protection existed. When we put the product in the grocery store, it was right in front of that mother, who surely was concerned about her child's welfare. We literally built the repellent

Johnson Wax entered the paint business with the introduction of Wax-o-Namel, a paint fortified with wax.

Johnson's entered the hair care business in 1977 with Agree, memorably targeted to young people to help them fight the "greasies." This was followed up with the Enhance line in 1980 and the Halsa line in 1984.

Scubapro

Minn-Kota Motors

Old Town Canoe, Eureka Tent, Johnson Reels, Silva Compass

Beginning in 1970, sensing a need for additional growth opportunities because older markets were maturing, the company launched a full-scale search and acquisition program, spanning eight years, in the leisure time businesses. This effort resulted in the acquisition of seventeen companies called the Johnson Wax Associates. In 1986, Sam Johnson and his family purchased the subsidiary to enable the parent company to concentrate on core business.

market, of which Off!™ now enjoys over a sixty-five percent share in United States. Today the market totals $60 million in the U.S. alone.

We recently entered the personal care field, with products such as shampoos and hand lotions. The technology of the personal care line is not all that different from what we have been doing for years; the emulsions, cleaners, and perfumes are somewhat the same. Moreover, because of our work with insecticides, we understand human toxicology. Therefore, personal care products was a natural path for us to follow.

In the 1970s, however, we undertook a rather different diversification tack, purchasing fifteen companies related to the outdoor recreation business. The spate of acquisitions really is a remarkable collection of case studies, running the gamut of winning and losing when buying other firms. But the net of it all is that we had a profitable $100 million outdoor recreation business. In 1986, my family and I purchased the subsidiary operating this end of the business. This purchase enabled the parent company to concentrate its management expertise on our core businesses and businesses closely allied to them. It also allowed the family liquidity when we took it public in 1987. Johnson Worldwide Associates has grown to $250 million in sales and is quite profitable. The stock has risen on the market and it operates independently of Johnson Wax, even though it is family-controlled. It adds great flexibility to family estate planning because of access to the public market, and it may offer alternative career opportunities to the next generation.

To sum up, the primary objective for a corporate leader is to ensure institutional survival. Developing a survival strategy is what every company and every CEO is doing. To survive you have to grow. To grow you have to diversify. Therefore, diversification is essential to survival.

When a company is diversified into various fields, it is rarely seriously vulnerable to the ups and downs that ravage individual businesses. And, if you are geographically diversified—that is, spread throughout the nation and the world—then you have some insulation between yourself and localized political and economic trouble.

Johnson Wax is today a company that is spread across many product lines and businesses. We are in international banking, overseas insurance, real estate, venture capital, and many other areas. Like the spider's web, there is far more strength in the interlocking fibers than in any single strand.

We could still be a small manufacturer of parquet flooring, but diversification has given us solid prospects for long-term survival and success.

CREATIVITY

"Having a creative climate that rains no retribution for bad ideas is one that nurtures the good and practical notions."

Creativity, I'm convinced, is an important element that has helped set our company apart from others. I think that in the beginning it was a fairly creative notion on the part of my great-grandfather that put Johnson Wax in business. A floor maker by trade, he saw a business opportunity with an idea that was rather simple, but that others were missing.

In his day, about 99 percent of the floors in America were shellacked. Yet shellac was a pretty bad material. It frequently chipped and easily wore off. To get a floor looking halfway decent you had to remove the shellac with a solvent and start all over again. Floors were often marred, if not ruined, during attempts to remove the material, and people were forced to sand it off, a tedious and difficult chore.

My great-grandfather recalled that there were castles in France with wood floors which had been treated with wax and had lasted for three hundred years. And, he applied this recollection to his knowledge as a floor maker. By making that intellectual transition, the essential connection, he was on his way to devising a product that became Johnson's Prepared Wax.™ It was quite a leap from making floors to creating an all new way to care for them. While the idea may seem obvious today, it was not at the time. My great-grandfather's "discovery" was like so many ideas that seem so simple now, but were clearly novel and original in their time.

Seeing the significance of vital relationships is very much a part of the creative process and should be part of disciplined scientific training. Men and women with technical backgrounds can all of a sudden "see the light" and connect disparate thoughts. Take the example of Sir Alexander Fleming, who had spent a lifetime studying the microbiology of molds. While working with a particular kind of mold, Fleming discovered that germs would not grow near the little droplet of white liquid that developed near the mold. By sheer serendipity Fleming had found penicillin, a drug that we take for granted today, but that only fifty years ago represented a miracle. Fleming, of course, had a sensitivity to discovery. As a trained scientist, he could envision the significance of what he observed.

Prepared Paste Wax and then Prepared Liquid Wax were the first consumer products for the retail trade.

Another vital ingredient to creativity—especially creativity within a corporation—is an environment which encourages the process. My father was a creative sort. He was trained as a chemist, but he was well-rounded; he had cultural and artistic sensitivities. Sometimes he provided fine ideas. Perhaps more important, he could *recognize* good ideas.

Moreover, he challenged other people's creativity. He had a persistent approach: "Why don't you try this or that?" Challenging people is an essential part of fostering creativity. I like to think I have also contributed to this environment and to making Johnson Wax a place where creative thought can occur. It's an atmosphere of stimulation, challenge, debate, constructive criticism, humor, and a willingness to come up with unusual ideas that may work—or that may be so sublimely ridiculous that all of us, including the innovator, can laugh. Having a creative climate that rains no retribution for bad ideas is one that nurtures the good and practical notions. I hope the next generations of managers understand this vital ingredient of success.

Unfortunately, that kind of creative environment tends to fade as a company grows and becomes more bureaucratic. Very few major firms—with say, Hewlett Packard, 3M, and but a handful of others being notable exceptions—do a good job of fostering employees' creativity. At least most big companies don't do it as well as it could be done.

In past years, the technical aspect of a product idea seemed to be the easiest part of the job. Once you had a good idea—the overall concept for a product—it seemed you were almost always able to work it out from a technical point of view. This process was particularly smooth in the 1950s right up through the mid-1970s, the era of the marketing man. A company got its ideas from the consumer, then used existing technology to develop the product to fit the consumers' desires.

As we understand more and more about fundamental chemical,

physical, and biological structures and their interactions, we will see astounding technical breakthroughs. We will have to take those advances and figure out ways to use them and package them, to meet needs consumers don't yet even know they have.

The whole micro-electronics business—which has astounded us all by its progress—is really just beginning. There is also potential for a tremendous wave of new products of one kind or another that will come from bio-engineering and genetic engineering. Our increased understanding of the nature of life, both plant and animal, creates a whole new environment for product development.

I am not certain how we get these two corporate forces—the modern technologist and the savvy marketing man—together. I think this is one of management's greatest challenges. Today, more than ever, the emphasis is on technology as the backbone of any product. We need always to enhance—or sometimes, renew—our technical creativity.

There are many solutions to problems that can be discovered only by leaps of creativity. And creativity is basically this: making connections between disassociated ideas and forces, and coming up with a combination which is distinctly different.

Business is a competition for the best ideas that create a market, meet consumer needs, and/or attack an emerging problem. Such was the case with Raid House and Garden, Flea Killer, and Brite Clean & Shine for no-wax floors.

Creativity obviously takes many forms. Artists are generally considered creative individuals, as are those who write music. And while one may have distinctly differing views on the relative merits of Beethoven's symphonies and the melodies of a popular rock group, each in its own way is creative. Both move listeners to a higher level of emotion.

All creative people, be they architects, novelists, filmmakers, scientists, or businessmen, have a common talent: they put disparate elements together to make something new.

It's important to recognize that everyone can be more creative. I think we all have multiple directions in which we can travel. Educational background, health, or one's origins can have little to do with being creative. Tchaikovsky was trained to be a lawyer, yet he was one of the greatest musical composers ever. Louis Pasteur, the famed French chemist and bacteriologist, was originally trained in art.

Age need not make a difference: Mozart was writing music before he was five, and Grandma Moses stormed the art world at the tender age of eighty. Frank Lloyd Wright, whose creative genius enlivened our offices and buildings in Racine, had a great comment about creativity and old age. "In the creative mind we have a fountain of energy that does not dry up as bones become brittle and the hair shines whiter, or thinner . . . or not at all. Any work of any lifetime, truly animated by principle, will leave fresh ideas upon the drawing boards in the morning. We speak of immortality—it lies here and now and is found in this quality we call creativity."

Nor need health make a difference. Beethoven was stone deaf when he wrote some of his last greatest works. Galileo's scientific insight was not dimmed by blindness late in life.

Intelligence may be helpful, but measured intelligence, like the numbered result of an IQ test or performance in school, doesn't always mean a lot. Einstein was considered a sluggard as a youth. William Faulkner didn't make it through high school. Nor is one limited by geography. Alexander Bell perfected the first working telephone in a small town in Ontario, Canada, and the Mayo Brothers built their famous clinic in the small town of Rochester, Minnesota.

How do we become creative? First, we have to be open-minded, to be predisposed to creativity. Second, we can't be negative. It's easy to criticize the new, but it's hard to notice what's basically good about a new idea. One has to look past the rough edges and see the core, the central part of an idea and how it might be refined into something good.

Third, we must be sensitive and perceptive, which means soaking up lots of impressions and facts, and seeing through the eyes of an artist, the emotions of a poet, the touch of a sculptor, and the mind of a scientist. As Dr. Carl Rogers said, "The mainspring of creativity is evident in all human life. It awaits only the proper conditions to be released."

Any one of us at any time can start establishing these proper conditions, for they are clearly under our control. They are internal. External factors cannot blunt creativity, if we are willing to fire our inside enthusiasm. One must be experimental, piece disassociated things together, and envision the product. It may be something great. But patience is often required. Epictetus said: "No great thing is created suddenly—any more than a bunch of grapes or a fig. If you tell me that you desire a fig, I answer that there must be time—let it first blossom—then bear fruit—then ripen."

Creative thought is the interplay between logic and inspiration, an interchange between the left and right sides of the brain. One has to tune into both parts of the thought process. It may seem mystical or difficult, but it's not.

Television journalist Bill Moyers hosted an excellent public broadcasting series on creativity a couple of years ago in which he said that the elements of creativity can be boiled down into seven notions. First, says Moyers, we must ask "Why?" Second, we should recognize patterns, and third, see the similarities between different ideas or events. Fourth, we should note new ways of seeing the strange as familiar, and the familiar as strange, and from there start making connections between the two. Fifth, we must take risks and not be fearful of being wrong. Sixth, we should use chance to our advantage, as Charles Goodyear did in taking advantage of the unexpected with the vulcanization of rubber. Seventh, we should establish networks to exchange ideas and questions with others. We feed on one another's creativity, and it certainly helps to "stand on the shoulders of others."

There is in our business a pressing need for more creativity. Our company must redouble its efforts to encourage, watch for, and act upon the creative efforts of individuals. When we were a small company, ideas were not only discussed, but also captured and used. In a large organization, unfortunately, ideas can get lost.

Contemporary management philosophy holds that business is becoming a competition for the best ideas. This is especially evident in the technological areas of industry. A good example is the American automobile industry, which lost its creative drive, and only now is it beginning to come back. For too many years U.S. car makers thought they had it all together, contenting themselves with building autos which were bigger and went faster, were more comfortable, had fins, or didn't have fins. On the whole, auto executives just plain overlooked creative changes in the technology of the production process.

The Japanese, on the other hand, used computers capable of car design. They forged ahead on the science of robotics, and applied it to automobile manufacturing. They pushed a number of unrelated ideas and forces into the car business, and essentially clobbered Detroit. We will, I believe, catch up after a period of serious soul searching and renewing our goals for the business.

At Johnson Wax we cannot afford to lose any creative thought, no matter what level or area it comes from. Creativity is the foundation of our "Product Plus" concept. It is the essence of the company's future. A creative thought launched this enterprise. The lack of a creative atmosphere could slow it down. But we are committed to a creative future.

RESEARCH AND DEVELOPMENT—THE ROLE OF TECHNOLOGY

"Companies that have led in the technology of the 1980s are the ones that are going to establish the foundations for future success."

Research and development at Johnson Wax had its beginnings in the early 1900s, when our first lab group consisted of three people. Today our R & D efforts involve more than 800 people worldwide and nearly 540 at world headquarters. One-half of the R & D staff hold degrees representing the disciplines of chemistry, polymer science, entomology, microbiology, biochemistry, pharmacology, physics, and engineering. Our worldwide R & D staff is widely recognized for its contributions to polymer chemistry, aerosol technology, finishes and coatings, insect control and behavior, and innovative packaging.

But our beginnings were quite humble. My great-grandfather was not a chemist: he was a merchant, and so was my grandfather. They did not know much about chemistry, but they got advice here and there, mixed trial formulas, and came upon a few floor wax formulations that worked pretty well.

As I said before, the early experiences with waxes and auto products taught my grandfather that chemistry was required in his new business. So my father (H.F.) joined the company as our first-ever chemist. Not long afterwards the company hired a PhD in Chemistry from the University of Wisconsin to become S. C. Johnson's first research director, Dr. J. V. Steinle.

My father was always the champion of technology throughout his career. He believed in product quality—the "Product Plus" concept— and in the value of science and technology both in the laboratory and in manufacturing. He knew that research was an important ingredient to company success.

For many years my father personally interviewed all the new chemists and engineers we hired. When he had his stroke and could no longer run the business, I have a sense that our corporate

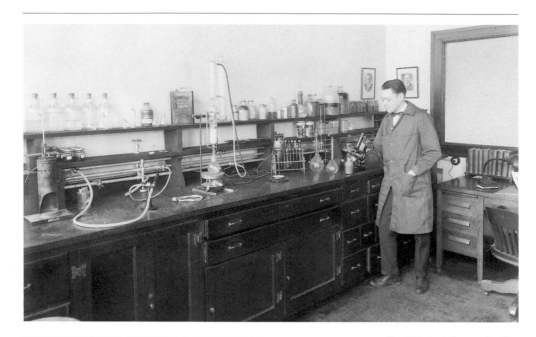

Dr. J.V. Steinle was the first professional chemist hired by the company. He is shown in his "lab" in 1925.

Fragrances play in important part in many products produced by Johnson Wax, none more important than in air fresheners. Chemist Donald E. Erickson appraises samples in a Glade test.

technology waned. While I had minored in chemistry at Cornell, I felt more comfortable as a professional manager. In the scheme of things, then, technology decreased in importance as advertising and marketing became our watchwords.

The late 1960s and early 1970s were the heyday of the marketing man. Chemists and researchers became helpers in the business, rather than the principal actors moving the company toward still further success. As a business enterprise, we were still living off the technological advances developed in the 1950s and early 1960s. In the last few years, however, I have come to the conviction that the era of the marketing man, while not over, has been nudged aside by the need for research, development, and new technologies. The preeminence of marketing as the basic skill that ensures success in business has been matched by technology. Companies that have led in the technology of the 1980s—a truly exploding technological era—are the ones that are going to establish the foundations for future success in product development and market share.

But to be successful, companies must develop a coordinated strategy for both technological development and marketing. To grow, companies must find new markets and new customers for existing products, as well as develop new products for both current and new markets and customers. Johnson Wax has shown its ability to do this by moving from floor care to car care to skin care products and from natural raw materials to synthetics.

This kind of coordination between R & D and marketing requires extensive communication and interaction between groups of executives and scientists. In the future these two primary forces must work as an integrated partnership jointly with manufacturing to bring new technological developments quickly forward, ahead of the competition. In the past, when marketing was supreme, our marketing people would identify consumer needs and wants and recommend the development of new products. Now, as our research and development people develop new technologies, we must find or create new markets or niches to use them. We encourage our research personnel to explore new product concepts and to develop them to the point where team effort can quickly bring these concepts to the product development stage.

Product modification resulting from communication between scientists and the marketers is essential to keeping on top of the highly competitive and rapidly changing consumer market.

What might seem a rather mundane research task—coming up with a nice new fragrance for a shampoo or an air freshener—actually calls upon state-of-the-art chemistry. Our scientists, along with a professor at the Medical College of Wisconsin and researchers at Nicolet Instrument Company in Madison, are working in "Fourier transform ion resonance mass spectroscopy," a revolutionary technique for identifying complex molecules in ultra-low concentrations (nanomoles). This new technology, when coupled with gas chromatography, allows us much greater accuracy and speed in analyzing fragrances. The fragrance from a single flower blossom or fruit can be shown to contain from ten to fifty components, each of which can be identified. The whole process, which not long ago would have required years of work on many pounds or even tons of flowers or fruit, now can be accomplished in a few hours.

It is at the Louis Laboratory, Johnson's central R & D facility among a number of others around the world, that Johnson Wax scientists conduct research in the major areas of our business—hair care, skin care, floor polishes, insect control compounds (attractants, repellents, cidal compounds, pheromones, growth hormones), furniture care products, air fresheners, laundry products, and, most recently, health care products. These labs, completely renovated in 1982, provide the best facilities possible for doing advanced research and development.

The operation and organization of our laboratories are especially important, because we want to provide an atmosphere where scientists enjoy the pleasure, recognition, and satisfaction from working in their fields of specialization, as well as from being an integral part of a dynamic, market-oriented company. To do this, they must be given the time and freedom to be creative, innovative, and imaginative. This is not always easy to accomplish, because historically many of the great advances in science have been made by individuals who are basically unconventional and sometimes difficult to manage. Good scientists often do not fit into a corporate structure. Therefore, it is important to have scientist-administrators who appreciate the technical contribution of such individuals and can integrate them into the whole. Also, all those involved in laboratory experimentation should be relieved of as much administrative burden as possible.

Some recent advances in science and technology have been made because of widespread concerns about the environment. This is certainly true in the development of our aerosol technology, which anticipated environmental concerns and proved to be a pioneering effort in the industry. The new formulations which we were obligated to develop actually led to lower-cost products, as the result of the introduction of cheap hydrocarbon propellants. Safety is another important incentive for scientific and technological development at Johnson Wax. Enormous efforts are expended on researching the toxicology of insecticides and repellents used in Raid™ products, fragrances in Glade,™ polymers used in printing inks for food packaging, and surfactants and emollients used in skin lotions, shampoos, and conditioners. Most of such "tox" testing is done under contract with specialized laboratories external to our own. Some product safety questions are answered in our own labs: for example, which design of a Shout™ bottle closure would best ensure against accidental ingestion by a child, or what design of a "bubble pack" air freshener will best resist puncture by a child armed with a ballpoint pen?

Concentration on specific scientific and technical applications has also proved an effective means of maximizing our R & D efforts. For example, polymers and polymer research have been extremely important in the development of our company. Our ability to develop and apply polymer technology has been a major factor in keeping us out front in the floor polish business. Today we are using polymers in a variety of other products and will be using even more in the future.

The researchers in our polymer labs refer to their work as "directed" basic research, some of which is long-term. The objective is to build a proprietary technology base from which a variety of applications can be derived.

For example, we developed our natural polymer, water-emulsion technology in the very early 1930s and are still using it. We developed Pride™ furniture polish based on silicone polymers, and that led to our very successful Pledge™ in the 1950s. Pledge™ is still a very important product for us.

A single technology can generate innumerable products. One example of how the internal development of a proprietary technology can lead to a burgeoning variety of spin-offs is illustrated below, which diagrams the history and future of polymer science and technology at Johnson Wax. The company began with the development of floor finishes. New materials were introduced to supplement the natural waxes which were first used, and two types of polymer systems were

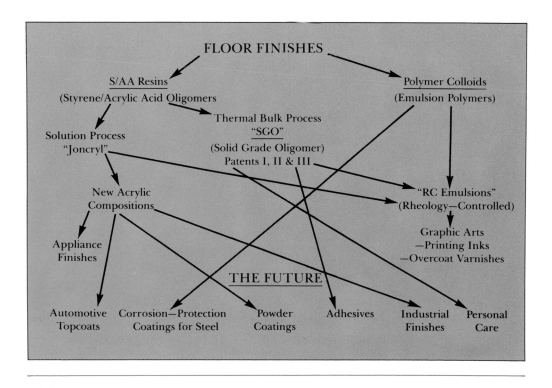

developed: styrene/acrylic acid (S/AA) oligomers and polymer colloids. These were combined in floor finish formulations to produce a formidable array of performance properties. Subsequently the decision was made to manufacture the S/AA polymers in-house, which in turn led to two manufacturing processes, a solution process and an "SGO" process, bulk thermal polymerization.

The bulk thermal polymerization process is capable of producing polymers low in molecular weight, narrow in molecular weight distribution, and in an almost infinite variety of compositions. As a result of having that capability, R & D was able to expand quickly into other polymer compositions, some of which were combined with the polymer colloid technology to form Johnson's Rheology-Controlled or "RC" emulsions. With research and development, marketing, and manufacturing capabilities in hand, Johnson could then begin to sell these polymer systems to others. The results have been highly profitable, initially in the graphic arts and more recently in the appliance finishes industries. New applications continue to become apparent, and vigorous projects are under way to develop polymer systems for automotive top coats, corrosion protection coatings for steel, powder coatings, adhesives, and industrial finishes as well as for personal care products. These are part of the Specialty Chemicals business, growing at the rate of seventeen to twenty percent per year.

Not all technological developments are as remote to the layman as research in polymer chemistry seems. Even the simple caps used on our products require sophisticated research and development. The fact that people do not think twice about a cap is testimony to the success of our product design.

Each cap design assignment contains two major objectives—one functional and the other aesthetic. The caps must be simple to use but distinctive enough to stand out on a supermarket shelf. Ideally, a cap should be functional, contemporary, efficient, and cost-effective. Consumers should feel they are getting a superior delivery or dispensing system, but that they have not spent extra money in getting it. The cap should not only be safe, it should look safe. Finally, it should be as convenient to store as it is to use.

A cap also presents complex production requirements. The cap design must be such that it can be produced and assembled with automated equipment, and, of course, it must be compatible with the product. To accomplish all this requires the coordinated efforts of our product design section, package engineers, materials engineers, tool engineers, manufacturing engineers, and product evaluation staff.

Important as it is, and complex as it is, cap design and manufacture do not fit most people's images of high technology. When people talk about technology these days they often think about computers. At Johnson Wax we have two creative computer applications to help the company streamline very different operations. One is in Component Engineering and the other is in the Distribution Department.

There are still other examples of how a strong technology base can lead to a number of spinoff products. In the 1950s Glade™ air fresheners and Raid™ insect sprays, and in the 1970s the personal care field, represented new technologies for us. The technologies we developed in these areas have served us well and will continue to do so, not only in the United States but throughout the world in our more than forty-five subsidiaries.

In Design Engineering, computer technology has brought drafting and design work, previously done manually on the drawing board, to the cathode ray tube (CRT). This computer-aided design/computer-

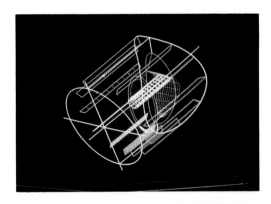

Computers help design engineers "test" options quickly. Dan Andersen, technologist, works on a Glade air freshener cap, analyzing design alternatives.

aided manufacturing (CAD/CAM) allows us to skip many steps in the design procedure and to complete many jobs in about one-half the time required with other methods. Once a sequence is programmed and the parameters are established, the system computes and constructs the geometry as many times as we need in order to test variables in specific design.

An important recent innovation goes even further in combining both artistic freedom and complexity with computerization. The designer creates a three-dimensional model of the desired piece in wood, clay, or plastic foam; a modification of the CAM then uses a special stylus to follow the contours of the model. This is converted to digital data, which can then be sent to the CAD to produce engineering drawings and instructions back to the CAM for milling prototypes and making molds. In time, the CAD/CAM group will be able to talk, computer-to-computer, by cable or satellite with Johnson Wax suppliers and subsidiaries throughout the world.

Another example of research and development at Johnson Wax is in the area of speciality chemicals, a group of products which evolved from the company's floor finish research in the 1950s. Today "Spec. Chem." provides some of our best and most innovative products. The

Electron microscopy has played an important role in studying surface properties and physical characteristics of insects. The current scanning electron microscope has taken such views as the staphylococcus bacteria (x 23,000) on an environmental surface and a mosquito's proboscis under similar magnification.

An RCA Transmission Electron Microscope in the 1950s was one of the first units of its kind to be installed in an industrial laboratory in Wisconsin.

speciality chemicals business produces polymer intermediates, synthetic compounds used in the formulation and manufacturing of inks, paints, adhesives, and coatings. These products are sold in large quantities under the brand name of Joncryl.™ They do not come in small bottles, cans, or jars, and you will not see them advertised in consumer magazines, on television, or in newspapers. However, our polymer products are among the most technically advanced in the world.

In the early 1960s we were conducting research on water-based polymer systems. Because polymers are an essential component of any protective coating such as our modern floor "polishes," and because they can carry color, inks were a natural place for us to enter new markets. Most inks at that time were made with solvent-based polymers, primarily because solvents dry faster than water, an important attribute that allows printing presses to print faster. At that time, solvent systems also produced a quality that was superior to their water-based counterparts.

A swarm of biting flies looks for a tasty morsel, but there's no bite on the arm of researcher Dave Bybee, who is evaluating a new repellent at the Biology Center.

Solvents, however, are released into the air as the ink dries and can therefore create a hazardous workplace as well as contribute to environmental pollution. Increasing air and water pollution problems became big news in the 1960s and early 1970s. In response, the Environmental Protection Agency (EPA) and Congress began ordering increased control on the release of solvents. As a result, water-based inks and coatings gained considerable attention.

However, it was not until the oil embargo in 1974 that water-based polymers really stepped into the limelight. The oil embargo caused solvent costs to spiral upward. Combined with stricter EPA rules on released solvents, these two external factors gave our products their most important new impetus in the marketplace. Because we had a tested and proven technology base, we were ready with a high quality product and a production capability to make it.

The development of this part of our business represents a good example of how a commitment to research and development, excellence in marketing—and some luck—can lead to a group of products with dramatic growth. Our speciality chemicals polymers area, while still small, is one of our most profitable and rapidly growing areas. For the future, we see expanded possibilities for the technological developments in genetics, engineering, and the physical sciences to be applied to new materials, processes, and products.

Not all of our commitment to research and development is in tangibles such as advanced equipment, though. In many ways I think it is the intangibles which are most important to success. At Johnson Wax we have the advantage of being in a small community, in an almost campus-like climate. Marketing people can walk around the labs and our research and development people can talk informally with marketing groups whenever the need arises.

Johnson Wax is a family company. We are in business for the next generation, not the next month's or next year's bottom line. We will continue to spend money on R & D and will continue to do it consistently, which is the only way to go. We cannot first be in and then out; you cannot turn research off and on like a faucet. It must be nurtured and encouraged before it can flourish.

NEW PRODUCTS—THEY MUST HAVE A "PLUS"

"Quite simply, you have to have new products—good products—or you die as a company."

Malcolm Forbes, the publisher of the magazine that bears his name, has told of the time when he was fresh out of college and running a small weekly newspaper in Lancaster, Ohio. He and his father were invited to tour a glass company, the largest employer in town. The founder of the firm took the pair through the company's lab. "We usually don't show this to anybody," said their host, "because what we have here are products that five years from now will account for eighty percent of our sales. Yet none of these things are we now making."

Young Forbes was impressed at the foresight. "They knew," he said, "that they were not going to be selling tomorrow what they were making today." And it is also true in our businesses, where most existing products can be expected, over the course of time, to be pre-empted by other new and improved products. Or, as similar products enter the market, to degenerate into a price-competitive situation, which yields narrow profit margins. Only by continually bringing forth new products, or improving upon old ones, can a company sustain long-term growth and profitability.

In 1984, 1,044 new products were introduced for food store distribution; however, various surveys have shown that from fifty to ninety-eight percent of all new products are downright failures. Time and again the same fundamental gaffe is made in the introduction of a new product: it simply isn't any better than what is already on the market. These mistakes are usually made by firms that are least able to bear the financial weight of the error.

It is for this reason that our company holds fast to a philosophy we call "Product Plus." In some ways it's a nebulous concept. During practically every Johnson Management Institute session we hold, the notion of Product Plus and what it means draw spirited debate, and the whole thing has to be re-explained.

In its most basic terms, a new item that carries Product Plus is one that has a distinct advantage over anything else on the market or is

so new that it faces no competition. It is also a product that clearly
has superior performance, with the difference readily apparent to
any consumer.

Minor technical superiority that the consumer can't recognize is not
true Product Plus. And while the consumer thinks it's a plus if the
new product is a money saver, that in itself doesn't meet our highest
standards. Though under certain circumstances an important cost and
price advantage can be the Product Plus, a true Product Plus item has
to be a breakthrough, with a performance edge over competitive
products that is visible to any consumer.

I didn't invent this concept. I remember well how it was instilled in
me by my father, who put great emphasis on the idea of making sure
you employ the best technology of whatever business you were going
into. I had just become the company's New Products Director, and our
section had decided that the insecticide field was a good and growing
business, one in which we wanted to play a part. So, I had a mock label
created, stuck it on a can, brought the sample of "Johnson's Aerosol
Insecticide" to my father, and announced that this was a business we
surely ought to enter.

He looked at me, and then at the can. "Don't you realize we don't
make any products without wax in them?" he asked.

Although H.F. was the boss, he was also my father, so I was able to
risk a little impertinence. "Well," I answered, "we could put a little wax
in it, but I don't think it would do the product any good."

My shot at humor didn't throw him off track. He told me we didn't
know anything about bugs. I replied that we were learning. "OK,"
he said, "then let's get down to fundamentals. Tell me what's better
about that product you're holding than what's already out there on
the market."

"It will have a nice label and be an aerosol," I offered.

"There are already a lot of aerosol insecticides with nice labels out
there," he said. "I've seen them."

"But we've got the Johnson label on ours," I explained. "And it works."

He wasn't about to give sway. "Does it work *better* than the other ones?"

"No," I admitted. "But there are all kinds of small companies, like
the one in Kansas City that makes Realkill, that don't have national
distribution like Johnson. We'd wipe them out."

"Come on now, Sam," he said, relentless in making his point. "Tell
me what is really better about this product."

Finally I caved. "If you really want to know, Dad, nothing. It's just a
darn good aerosol insecticide."

"Then take it back to the lab, and when you have got something
better, come back and we'll talk about the insecticide business."

A major diversification came when the company introduced a product not related to wax—Raid. Sam Johnson (right) did a lot of convincing to his father that this new product indeed had a Product Plus.

His instincts were right, and when we did come back with a better insect killer, it was Raid™ House & Garden Spray, the original insect killer that could be used on flying insects and plant insects. And when we came out with an aqueous formula, we indeed had a Product Plus. It smelled better and it would kill insects on plants without harming the plants.

Quite simply, you have to have new products—good products—or you die as a company. This is a reflection of our society, where people expect and demand progress. Consumers, of course, buy certain items out of loyalty and habit, but they also are on the alert for new and improved products that make life easier. When such developments are offered, an average consumer is quick to abandon loyalties. There is nothing wrong with this, for it puts pressure on business and industry to make better products, which ultimately boosts the quality of life for all citizens.

While it may seem that there is no room for improvement with some products, this is never really true. With creativity and innovation, there can almost always be beneficial product and packaging changes, which make the item perform at a higher level or give the consumer a stronger measure of satisfaction.

Take the pure commodities, such as sugar and wheat. Sugar was simply sugar, but along came Sucryl, saccharin, and a whole new generation of sweeteners, such as Aspartame. Wheat was wheat, but now genetic engineering techniques promise major modifications in the growing of that crop. Innovation is always possible: one just has to get an entire company thinking within the proper frame of reference. So if anyone ever says there's no space for innovation—in any business—I answer *baloney*!

There is, however a difference between innovation and the Johnson concept of Product Plus. Creating a pack of twenty-five cigarettes when all other brands have twenty is an innovation, but unless it is remarkable in another way it is not a Product Plus.

We've occasionally been guilty of kidding ourselves on the Product Plus issue, when all we've really had was a development that gave us a small edge in product positioning. In our experience those brands don't last very long—you get chewed up by your competition pretty quickly, or the brands drift off into minor market shares.

Over the years I've become convinced that while positioning and market segmentation are very important, the products themselves must establish that position, with a unique attribute that fits the position.

Sam Johnson, second from left, organized the New Products Department for Johnson Wax in 1954-55, an innovative organization that became a model for other companies.

Take our traditional floor wax business, where we have four brands positioned for women who have certain kinds of floor care problems. While the old Glo-Coat™ has become a rather ordinary product these days, it is a "price pointed" product. Moreover, since it has some traditional value as well, it has had a following for many years.

The floor covering and floor care business in recent years has produced novel coverings that their manufacturers say need only a no-wax cleaner. For some reason this development crept up on us before we recognized a need for a new product. So, we scrambled, and developed a polymer that gave a shine to no-wax floors. Brite™ was absolutely a terrific product. We thought we had ourselves a tremendous Product Plus. Rushing through tests, we did the usual multiple coating tests and things like that; despite R & D findings that there may be crazing and whitening problems with multiple applications, we rushed it to market.

Consumers agreed on the excellence of Brite,™ and it swiftly grabbed a sixteen percent market share. People liked it so much they were using it at least once a week, if not more. And then, after about three months, the consumers, just like our R & D experts predicted, began noticing the crazing and whitening problems.

We decided to reformulate the product, re-label it, and go back out and get that market. The market was there, but we had to have the Product Plus to capture it. We came up with a fine looking new label and called it New Brite.™ We started all over with our advertising. We said you could put on multi-coats, hundreds of them, and it wouldn't cause floor problems. It didn't, for New Brite™ worked.

The New Brite™ experience reinforced an excellent lesson: there are cases when you shouldn't give up on a brand. By the time we came out with New Brite,™ most of the old stuff was off the shelf. Now our share is back up to nineteen percent.

The ability to anticipate the needs of the consumer is an essential ingredient found in *the* successful, innovative company. Market anticipation requires hard work. You must go after it, because it does not come easily. The leadership in a company must head the drive to foster anticipation; it just doesn't happen naturally. Other companies have made errors like those made on Brite™ by not having foresight. While the Brite™ experience didn't wreck our overall business, similar miscues have nearly destroyed companies. A classic example is Schlitz.

Schlitz had tried marketing a light beer ten or fifteen years ago, but it didn't sell well. The market simply wasn't ready for light beer. But about the time people became conscious of keeping their calorie intake down, Miller introduced their light beer. Schlitz, working off their previous experience, didn't believe the light concept would work, and

The development of Pledge with its promise of "waxed beauty instantly" was an R & D breakthrough. It was a novel, pressurized, silicone water/wax emulsion system, with dramatic performance characteristics that captured the hearts of consumers, who made it the number-one furniture polish.

In 1970, Johnson Wax came out with something R & D had long sought—Future, a clear floor care product in a package which would enhance its unique characteristics in the eyes of consumers.

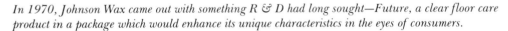

Edge shaving gel was the company's entry product in the personal care market and drew a loyal consumer following that made it to the top of the charts in face of strong competition.

Curel, a therapeutic lotion which ends dry skin, was an important advance in the personal care line.

didn't come out with a counter product until they were nearly bankrupt.

You just cannot give up on a product, especially when it shows promise for being a Product Plus. I regularly go through New Products Review sessions; at each session the R & D group has come up with some good things, better than the year before. My regular comment at the end of these sessions is, however, "Think about the innovations in fields where we tried and failed, because maybe today there is another way that we can crack those markets."

Technology and ideas, to be sure, feed on themselves, if you know enough to put disparate parts together. I recall the Befresh™ toilet bowl cleaner and deodorizer we developed, but which flunked the test. It was to be clipped on the inside of the bowl, but it just didn't work. Then I noticed that another firm was coming out with a new in-tank product that had two different chemicals being metered out at the same time, one a bleach and the other a deodorant. It was a good idea. So, I told our people to take another look at that business, to look for a way that we could do it better.

I also wanted them to revisit the carpet business, for we missed the whole deodorant part of the carpet-cleaning market. We didn't think there was anything there. Glory™ rug cleaner still hangs in there with a little piece of the market, but there has got to be something we can do for carpets that is bigger and better.

Nevertheless, we are doing a good job of innovating in the insecticide business, primarily through line extensions. We are coming out with insecticides for insects that few people worried about, among them fire ants and fleas. Fleas will invade homes that have no pets and bite people. So we've got a spray that is effective in flea control.

Fire ants have been creating problems throughout the American Southwest, and fleas are a perennial scourge. Environmental Protection Agency regulations have prohibited wide spraying, and the bugs are winning. So, insecticides are a marvelous business to be in, and we are innovating very effectively.

And, of course, there are other very effective applications we have made of new technologies, like residual pyrethroids, smoke in Raid Fumigator,™ and IGR's in Flea Killer Plus.™

A superior innovation, something with Product Plus, will win in the marketplace. It can even transcend a company's original positioning ideas. One such example is our Edge™ shaving cream, in particular our Special Edge™ version. Although Special Edge™ doesn't say "Black" on the label, it is heavily marketed and positioned in areas with large Black populations because of some special skin problems among males. It's also designed for people with sensitive skin. But it's so good, is so much more lubricious, and feels so different from any other shaving product, that it's now the largest seller in a six-item category.

Product Plus has to be an ethic, almost a company religion. But as I've explained, it's sometimes tough to judge whether a strong-selling product is doing well because of Product Plus, good advertising, a proper price point, or a combination.

When we came up with aqueous-based Glade™ air freshener, we were able to reduce its price by about forty percent. That put Glade™ into a whole different price category, and opened up the market in a way older and more expensive aerosols never would have done. Also, by being aqueous-based, it smelled better. We had a high quality product, we had more money to put into better perfumes, and we put it out there in the market at a lower price. Glade™ carried a double-whammy Product Plus and was an instant success.

Still, how can consumers judge technical superiority in products like shampoos and hair conditioners? How can one tell a minor performance difference? In some products, a small plus is readily apparent. Not in shampoos.

When your plus isn't large, you can make headway with advertising, good packaging, and positioning. Packaging is very important, for it can denote Product Plus inside. While the guts of the product are far and away the most important factor, design and aesthetics must always be major considerations. When we brought out our Agree™ shampoo, we recognized that young people often have a problem with greasy hair, while older people have dry hair. We positioned Agree™ for the younger market, saying in ads that it attacks the "Greasies." Agree™ is good for greasy hair. So what we've got is positioning and a Product Plus. But positioning itself won't work if the new product is ordinary and doesn't deliver the results you're touting.

Advertising flows out of Product Plus. The easiest advertising to write is that concerning a truly unique and better product. Agree™ wasn't quite as simple; its advantages over its competitors were not as great. Edge™ was fairly easy, particularly with the commercial where we had a credit card scraped across a face to show how close the Edge™ shave really was.

When you're paying $400,000 for thirty seconds of commercial time on something like the "Cosby Show," then you'd better have an important message in hand. Otherwise, you're wasting an awful lot of money. Mark Twain once said, "The difference between the right word and the almost right word is the difference between lightning and the lightning bug." But even with the appropriate words and a Product Plus, it's often hard to get the message across.

Ultimately this is what business is all about: building the better mousetrap again and again. American business and industry will have to keep coming up with better products if we are going to compete successfully against foreign firms. The Japanese have done well in television, for example, because many of their sets, like the Sony, are the best on the market. They cost more, but the quality is a premium consumers will pay for.

A small or minor Product Plus isn't going to be enough. Moreover, that plus can rapidly disappear when the competition catches up with you, as it invariably will. You always have to be thinking for the next Product Plus, even while you have a good one out there performing. You must be constantly thinking, exploring, and trying to figure what the next consumer need will be. And that, simply, is what makes the business so interesting.

ADVERTISING AND MARKETING—PUTTING A PRODUCT IN ITS NICHE

". . . most of the new thrusts in marketing over the next ten years are going to flow from technology."

Hundreds of products and services are being advertised today. Creative, compelling, and entertaining commercials crowd the airwaves, roadways, magazines, and newspapers. And many of the products touted in these advertisements—like a particular make of car or an advanced home computer—already have developed an intrinsic interest within the audience. The consumer is at least alert, if not completely receptive, to the message.

The products made by Johnson Wax don't often generate that kind of emotion. Audiences simply are not as attentive to advertising for certain consumer products, such as cleaners and polishes, as they might be to others, such as a new video cassette camera. Therefore, we have a more difficult time than some other companies with our advertising visibility. Although we do as good a job of advertising as anyone in our business, we can at times get lost in the clutter of television, radio, and print ads.

Given the assumption that our competition has advertising agencies just as good as ours, and that they can be just as much a part of the clutter as we, then the question we must answer becomes, "What will set Johnson Wax apart?" The answer, which is pretty obvious, is technology, the technology to make products with a genuine difference. You absolutely must have that special ingredient to separate yourself from the herd of advertisers, markets, and sellers of consumer products. I am convinced that technology is the only way to stand tall.

As we have found that sustaining our long-term growth depends on the development of new products or improved versions of existing products, our advertising and marketing efforts also must be attuned to the Product Plus philosophy. Product Plus has multiple payoffs in today's competitive marketplace:

1. It gives the salesperson a competitive edge because he or or she is representing a superior product.

2. It results in better advertising, because with a Product Plus you can make a distinctive claim, and often can back it up with a convincing demonstration.

3. It benefits the trade customer. The manager recognizes the innovation and realizes that the product belongs in the store.

4. It facilitates introduction of a new or improved product. Sustaining the Product Plus as an exclusive as long as possible can maintain the heavy selling which can result from a good product introduction.

Advertising agencies today play a much more dominant role in the marketing of a product than ever before. Such was not the case in the 1920s and 1930s, which really was the era of the salesman and corporate salesmanship. Sales drove the engines of consumer products companies. As the national media developed, first with magazines and then with radio, so did the role of advertising in helping a company become known and in moving its products.

This page from an 1892 Ladies Home Journal *includes one of the earliest of the company's national advertisements.*

Johnson introduced its line of car-savers, such as Carbon Remover and Freeze Proof just before the "Roaring Twenties" and advertised then in such national publications as Motor Age *and* Motor *(in Canada) (1917).*

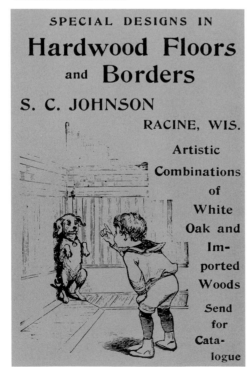

In one of broadcasting's longest sponsor relationships, "Fibber McGee & Molly" was on the air for fifteen years, helping to make Johnson's Wax and Glo-Coat household words.

In 1961, Red Skelton, whom Johnson Wax had sponsored on television since 1954, filmed one of his shows in the Great Workroom as part of the company's 75th Anniversary.

Standing out was much easier then, for if a company were connected with a hit radio program, its name would become nearly synonymous with the show. A few companies even had their names in the program title, like "Campbell Playhouse," sponsored by the soup company, or "The Voice of Firestone," backed by the tire and rubber firm. Today, because of the cost of television advertising, sole sponsorship of leading programs is virtually impossible. The average cost of a thirty-second spot is $200,000; some shows, like Cosby's, command $400,000! On any given hit series, a company like ours is most likely to be one of eight sponsors.

Johnson Wax became involved in radio advertising and program sponsorship quite early in the medium's life. It was a crucial decision, considering the relative unknowns surrounding radio, such as the questionable business acumen of barely formed networks and uncertain projections of audience size. Among the first shows sponsored by Johnson Wax were "The House by the Side of the Road" and "Ted Weems." But it was the "Fibber McGee and Molly" program that made the difference.

In the years following World War II, televison stole radio's thunder. The first time I saw a television, just a small screen at the RCA exhibit, was at the World's Fair of 1939. But that small screen grew to have incredible impact in an equally incredibly short period of time. By the 1950s, TV was the dominant news and entertainment medium.

The company went along with the trend. In fact, television actually was better than radio for Johnson Wax. With television, we could demonstrate the use of the product. In the early days of the tube, before the public was jaded by literally millions of hours of programming and visual images, product demonstrations were razzle-dazzle stuff. And what we discovered in the 1950s still holds true today—there is nothing as communicative to the consumer as a meaningful demonstration of the product.

For a time Johnson Wax had its own shows, or was the exclusive sponsor of Robert Montgomery and Red Skelton. However, as the networks expanded and grew stronger, the number of programs grew. Independent stations multiplied; the number of people viewing television multiplied. Audience loyalties to specific shows eroded. As the potential audience for television commercials expanded and changed, so did the financing and marketing strategies for television advertising. It became financially difficult, if not unwise, to concentrate advertising dollars in any one program. By spreading advertising across media and programs we found we could reach a greater audience.

However, as more and more companies followed this path, it became harder and harder to stand out in the crowd. In time, Johnson Wax no longer was a dominant part of radio or television. We were as strong as any advertiser in our markets, yet one among many. Another recent development in television advertising—the fifteen-second commercial—is presenting a new set of challenges to standing out in the crowd. Advertisers are going to be stretching their limits of creativity to get the message across and to have it memorable in fifteen seconds.

Cable television also is changing advertising. Like millions of other Americans, I spend a portion of my TV viewing time watching HBO, which carries no commercials (other than for itself). But marketers still have to reach the cable audience—on those stations carrying consumer ads—and they may do so with direct cable shopping. I believe that shopping via cable television will one day be favored by many people.

Consumers will be able to order many items shown on television, through purchasing systems much more sophisticated than we now find peddling record albums, vegetable slicers, and "miracle" fishing rods. Catalogs may also be showing us the way for additional possibilities in direct TV marketing. The proliferation of catalogs and the volume of catalog shopping have been practically unbelievable in the past few years.

Media advertising is not the only marketing tool we use, though. Sampling, for example, is one of the most expensive ways to enter a market, but in many ways it is the most effective. There are ways of holding down the cost and still realizing the benefits of sampling. If you give a sample of a superior product to only every third household, neighbors on either side will often find out how good it was by word of mouth. The product has to be significantly better than anything else, but if it is, the item will stand out from the clutter.

Marketing is indeed becoming increasingly diversified. There are many more ways to move a product—on television, through direct mail, and so on—than ever before. Moreover, one must increasingly target messages toward special interests.

Take the fortunes of the print media in recent years. I remember seeing Andrew Heiskell of Time, Inc. not all that many years ago, when he was chairman of the board, and when I asked him how he was doing, he said, "I feel like a man who is hanging onto the outside of the building with my fingertips." At that point *Life* had just folded, *Sports Illustrated* was struggling, and only *Time* was doing well. But that company has since revived *Life*, brought out magazines such as *People* and *Money*, and branched into cable television with HBO.

A major difference in publishing today versus twenty or thirty years ago is the decline of the general magazine, and the rise of many specialty books. The magazines that make money today are "target" publications, such as magazines for nurses, motorcycle buffs, and ultra-light aircraft pilots. Where there were once only two or three flying publications, six or seven now compete for the pilot's interest. The print business is going strong, but is scattered among the specialty markets.

This general trend—the growth of special interests—is of increasing importance in almost all marketing. It is what can be called "nichemanship," and involves the recognition here at Johnson that there is not just one market for floor waxes. There are several markets, and we have to be represented in each one of them.

As a nation we have become more heterogeneous in our habits, hobbies, recreation, and entertainment choices. This presents a very wide target for the marketer.

You can, however, draw a bead on certain groups. First off, you must design your product for a specific consumer or consumer

Don Pegler, creator of the well-known animated television Raid commercials featuring "almost-human" ants, bugs, and roaches, drew the portrait of Sam Johnson in 1982.

need and be sure there are enough such customers to sustain mass distribution. A company also must be able to reach customers with the product through several different means in order to enter the various niches.

New niches appear and develop, and it infuriates me when we don't spot them before anyone else does when they are within our own sphere of business. We didn't perceive the market for no-wax floors, and it took a competitor to show us that there was a market for no-wax floor cleaners. The market is now sizeable—a quarter of all households have some floors that require no wax.

As such flooring gets older, however, it needs a formula that restores brilliance. When we finally recognized this, we rushed to market with Brite.™ Our mistake was that we were not attuned to consumer attitudes. Had we recognized the new market from the start, and initially gone in with a sound product, we would have been that much more ahead.

Technology, and the good new products it breeds, must go hand in hand with marketing. A technological breakthrough makes your marketing and advertising job much easier. If, for example, the breakthrough allows you to use cheaper ingredients—and is a better product than the competition's to boot—then you can undercut the other side with superior goods *and* a lower price.

This happened with our Glade™ Mist aerosol air freshener, when we began using water-based propellant instead of solvent. It smelled better, it sold for thirty percent less than the competition's product (in a bigger can, no less), and it drove the then-leading freshener "Florient" right out of business. The type of marketing position we were able to achieve with a combination of technology and competitive pricing is difficult to defeat, and we still hold about forty-five percent of the aerosol air freshener business.

Technology was important in the 1960s and 1970s. It will be even more vital in the 1990s. Just as Silicon Valley is producing high-tech electronics, we are entering an era of producing and using high-tech chemicals. We can tailor molecules and polymers far better than we could ten years ago. We have analytical tools to know what we are looking at. We have developed, for example, a new polymer that can control the viscosity of paints and other substances far better than ever before.

I believe that most of the new thrusts in marketing over the next ten years are going to flow from technology. It is the technical side of the business that will generate most new ideas. Still, our technologists and marketers must work together, thinking in hard business terms, but allowing themselves to dream as well. Serendipitous discoveries are not out of the question. The little yellow "Post It" pads developed by 3M were the result of an accident, a new glue that failed to stick all that well. It is now a $300 million product that created its own niche in the marketplace. Johnson Wax, or any business, could use products like that.

THE WHOLE WORLD IS
A MARKET

*"We are, in a sense, ambassadors; we attempt, along with
our primary business mission, to set a positive example
of free enterprise."*

Very early in this century, when the Johnson family business was quite small, my grandfather had the vision to believe that his wax products could be sold not only in the United States, but in many other countries as well. Viewed in retrospect, the logic he followed was quite basic. There were, he reasoned, more people outside the U.S. than within it, and they were propagating at a much higher rate than Americans were. Therefore, he concluded, the market opportunity outside the country had to be great and certainly promised solid future growth.

This was a seemingly elemental conclusion, to be sure; however, in 1913, it was a wise perception. Far too few businessmen in those days gave much thought to selling their goods outside the U.S., or even trading with foreign sources. Except for commodities such as coffee and tea that didn't grow in this country, and a few products that grew in the U.S. but not elsewhere, relatively little American international trade flowed when compared to today's volume.

Yet my grandfather believed that if Johnson Wax could succeed in America, it could sell in other nations. The first country he thought of was the family's ancestral homeland, England. Of course in those days one just didn't take a nine-hour nonstop flight from Chicago to London. In the time before O'Hare and Heathrow you boarded a Chicago-bound train in Racine, transferred to a train headed for New York, and then waited for a ship to sail. The voyage across the North Atlantic involved nearly two weeks of elegant but not Concorde-swift travel.

Despite the distance and time involved in such an expedition, my grandfather made the journey and called on English retail stores. However, it sometimes took all of his Yankee resourcefulness to convince the skeptical British of the worth of his products.

He perhaps was at his best the day he visited one particular iron mongery, or hardware store, in London. My grandfather—who had a penchant for wearing white flannel suits—carried with him a sample of his product and wanted to demonstrate it for the store owner. Facing an obviously incredulous merchant, he made a bold proclamation: "This product will not only clean your floor," he boasted, "it will polish it so shiny that you could drag me across the floor and not see any dirt on the seat of my pants."

The store owner watched my white-suited grandfather polish the floor. When the polish dried and was buffed, my grandfather sat down on his bottom. The merchant, who must have been a patient fellow, took the American salesman by the feet and pulled him across the floor. My grandfather then stood, turned around, and displayed a clean backside. "I'll buy some," said the store owner, offering no further resistance.

Such salesmanship generated a lot of orders, and the size of the market appeared substantial as my grandfather lined up a number of

Sam Johnson served as Executive Vice President and was responsible for international marketing in 1964 when he called together key people in Europe to talk about growing challenges and opportunities.

Sam Johnson gets an assist from Minister Karlamov of the Soviet Chamber of Commerce in officially opening the Johnson Wax Exhibit in Moscow in 1973 to introduce the company and its products to trade groups in the Soviet Union.

The first overseas factory was in West Drayton, in London, England, in 1916, two years after the founding of the first subsidiary, in London's High Holborn. Today the British company is located at Frimley Green, outside of London.

wholesalers and formed the British company in 1914. However, as the first shipment of Johnson Wax was prepared to go overseas, the Great War erupted. The company's initial shipment of products was sunk by a German submarine.

The British business was built up little by little. Today the subsidiary is a major U.K. company, and because it has been around so long, many people believe it is an English native. The firm holds Royal Warrants to supply waxes and polishes to Her Majesty the Queen, a Royal Warrant from the Queen Mother, and a Royal Warrant for Goddard's silver polish.

From Great Britain the firm moved next to other Commonwealth countries. Johnson Wax went to Australia in 1917, a six-week trip by boat out of San Francisco. Next, and much closer, was Canada.

While establishing a headquarters office and factory in Canada, my grandfather started a tradition that still serves the company well,

Johnson Wax subsidiaries have headquarters that exhibit unique design and enduring quality. Shown are only a few of the outstanding examples in the forty-five countries in which Johnson Wax has operations; Italy above, New Zealand left, Japan below.

wherever in the world we are doing business. We place our operations in smaller towns that are near urban centers. Employees therefore have the benefits of a metropolitan area—in culture, services such as major banks, and the like—and at the same time can be a part of a smaller community.

This "policy," if you will, came about almost by accident. My grandfather decided to make an overnight train trip to Toronto, where he intended to receive some advice from bankers and representatives in the retail trade on where the company might locate. As was his custom after dinner, he went into the bar car. He sat down next to a gentleman, and over a few drinks together, my grandfather told him his mission. The man then identified himself as M. M. McBride, the mayor of Brantford, Ontario. As the two talked, it became apparent that Brantford and Racine had parallels between them that were astonishing.

Brantford, the mayor told my grandfather, had about 30,000 people, just a bit smaller than Racine. When the mayor talked of the Grand River running through his town, my grandfather told him of the Racine Root River. Brantford is about fifty miles from Toronto; Racine is sixty miles from Chicago. But perhaps the most important feature about Brantford was that my grandfather liked that man. The next morning, when the train stopped there, he told the mayor that he didn't need to go on to Toronto. "I'll just get off with you and let you show me the town."

The company has been an integral part of Brantford ever since, and this Canadian venture set a pattern that has been followed over the years. Frimley Green is about thirty miles outside of London. Our Europlant in Mijdrecht, the Netherlands, is about twenty-five miles from Amsterdam. Italian Johnson is in Arese, just outside Milan, and our French company is in Cergy-Pontoise, on the outskirts of Paris. It is a system that has worked well.

Establishing such operations in other nations was absolutely essential to our future. The company needs manufacturing facilities because its products are basically not very exportable, primarily due to the weight/cost relationship in waxes and cleaners. Since many contain ingredients such as solvents and water, it simply doesn't make sense to manufacture them several thousand miles from the ultimate market and pay unnecessary shipping charges.

There also were other benefits. By investing in manufacturing capabilities, Johnson fairly quickly became a part of almost every nation in which we had located. Being a part of a country is insurance against being booted out or treated unfavorably. When a country's government institutes protectionist policies favoring domestic firms—

as has often happened—a "local" company really cannot be frozen out. That's why Johnson's international business has flourished over the years. Being on the inside of a market almost always is preferable to being on the outside trying to get in.

What most nations want from foreign businesses, of course, is investment, indigenous manufacturing, and employment for their own people. Most non-Communist nations welcome Western business. So, we go where we are welcome. That is why the company is in such places as Indonesia, Egypt, Kenya, Chile, and even smaller nations. As long as it has enough people, a country is worth investing in. This is why about sixty percent of our business is overseas.

This strategy is not that bad for the future either, because it is an approach that most helps a host country. It provides local jobs, investment, a transfer of technology, and a transfer of management know-how. A company doesn't do all that simply by shipping export items, however needed they may be.

My grandfather believed that a community and a country alike should be better off because we were there. And what applies in Racine—putting more into the community than we take out—applies equally well in Frimley Green, Brantford, and Mijdrecht. While this sounds rather lofty and altruistic, it is also, as a purely practical matter, the best way to do business.

We've been forced out by only two countries, a rather remarkable record for an American multinational. And being tossed out of Cuba by Fidel Castro and Iran by the Ayatollah Khomeini is really no disgrace, particularly when we were accompanied by all other United States businesses. Nevertheless, the company has endured in such nations as Chile, when it was under a Marxist regime, and through roughly fifty changes of government in Argentina. Today we are in more than forty-five countries with our own operations.

A corporation, wherever it is, always has certain responsibilities: protecting the environment, treating employees with dignity, and conducting business with universal human values in mind. There are, however, additional responsibilities when a corporation is a guest in a foreign nation. First, you must strive to adapt yourself to the culture of the host country and to support the local culture. I also believe that corporations have an obligation *not* to interfere with the political affairs of a sovereign nation.

Perhaps one can influence the economic affairs of a country by providing jobs and products, and purchasing local raw materials. And perhaps one can influence politics by introducing policies such as profit sharing, which may run counter to the way the government believes employees should be treated. One need not preach the merits

This Austrian Johnson advertisement shows a range of products familiar to U.S. shoppers, but also some aimed to that market: oven cleaner, scouring pads, and laundry starch.

of profit sharing—it might just catch on anyway. The main thing is that we should not preach a particular political point of view.

An American corporation certainly can practice its own business philosophy in other nations. But when abroad, it is downright foolish for a company to practice American politics. We are, in a sense, ambassadors; we attempt, along with our primary business mission, to set a positive example of free enterprise. We cannot be involved in causes, except perhaps in an indirect and quiet way.

Take, for example, our activities in South Africa. Frankly, we in the company find the South African government's apartheid policy deplorable and morally unacceptable. We have publicly stated that we wish to be counted among the forces working for reform and change. Indeed, we are opposed to any form of discrimination, anywhere in the world.

Johnson Wax has been urged by groups in the U.S. and elsewhere to quit our business in South Africa. Because we have chosen to remain, there are people who undoubtedly assume that we are there only to earn a profit, coldly ignoring the inhumanity of apartheid in the name of business. But in reality, leaving South Africa would have little financial impact on the company—South Africa represents less than one percent of our consolidated worldwide sales.

Instead of leaving, we feel that we can be a more effective force against such oppression by continuing to operate in that nation in a way that would lead to the ultimate elimination of unfair or discriminatory employment practices. Moreover, we feel we can never abandon our company in South Africa or the Johnson Wax people who live there. Our commitment there, as elsewhere, is for the long term.

I am convinced that we have been forceful agents of social change. Enlightened American firms such as ours provide opportunity and training for South African Blacks, Coloreds, and Asians; Whites and non-Whites are paid the same wages for the same job. The health care, educational aid, housing, and community support American companies have given their employees far exceed what is done by the majority of South African corporations. We set an example, and in turn influence legislative and administrative decisions that have enhanced the status of non-White South Africans.

Johnson Wax pays a minimum wage in South Africa that is forty-three percent above the government's official level. All company facilities are fully integrated. Of the 150 South African employees, ninety-four are non-White. We have nearly two dozen non-Whites in managerial, supervisory, and professional positions. Our South

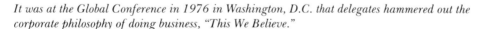

It was at the Global Conference in 1976 in Washington, D.C. that delegates hammered out the corporate philosophy of doing business, "This We Believe."

African employees all participate in profit sharing. We have two Black independent directors of South African Johnson and our Regional Vice President for Africa is a Nigerian.

Now, at the other extreme, there are countries in which we will adapt almost totally to *their* way of business. Our Japanese company is a good example. We have even borrowed certain Japanese management techniques and practices, such as placing the responsibility for quality with each person on the line, rather than with a quality control department at the end of the line.

No matter what form of management you ultimately follow, it is important to move into a country or potential market as early as you can. By doing this, you avoid having to fight entrenched competition of the type we faced in Italy after moving in late.

Following World War II, my father dispatched an executive to check on Italy. The cities were still bombed out, and the company's man thought it wouldn't be worth placing a Johnson operation there. He believed Italy might never make a comeback from the war. My father, on the other hand, was skeptical. Although he accepted the recommendation not to build a plant, he insisted we place a licensee in Italy.

When I went to Europe in 1959 to run operations there, one of the first places I visited was Italy. By then, the country had been rebuilt. I walked into a store and saw Colgate toothpaste and Lever detergents all over the place. We had missed it! Or, at best, we were late. Fortunately, however, our licensee was a capable man, and we quickly formed an Italian company, which today is very strong.

It was then that I vowed never to be late getting into a market. For years, Colgate's most profitable market outside the United States was in Italy. It took us all too long to go fully Italian when, with only a modest investment, we could have been a part of that country's postwar growth. It often is wise to start small, if only on the promise of grand dreams. This is one of the reasons we have not been shy about seeking business in the Soviet Union and the People's Republic of China.

As a true believer in free enterprise, I am not at all in agreement with Marxist philosophy. Yet there are millions, indeed more than a billion, Soviets and Chinese who are potential customers. We have tried to negotiate a joint venture with the Soviets, but they only want to buy technology: to have us build a plant and leave. However, we have sold them a considerable amount of products over the years. We think that a continuous relationship is absolutely vital to our way of doing business and have turned down alternative proposals.

The Chinese have been much more amenable to a joint venture, and we are successfully operating one there. Since the only way to do

THE WHOLE WORLD IS A MARKET

THE WHOLE WORLD IS A MARKET

Sam Johnson learned early on that cultural experiences were part of the world of an international businessman as evidenced by his visiting New Zealand in 1972, dancing the Tinikling on a trip to the Philippines in 1965, and meeting with Japanese managers in 1965.

95

business in any country is to have a solid and continuing relationship, we made the joint venture approach our one major precondition. Being a partner, or wholly owning the subsidiary, has already worked for nearly eighty years, and I think it will be just as valid eighty years from today.

Still, one must be aware that it is easy to make errors concerning a place thousands of miles from home. For roughly twenty-five years we lost money in Brazil. Not much, but we had to keep investing just a little more each year. It was partly our fault for not having the right kind of management. But we also fouled up by having a plant near Rio, a sales office in Sao Paulo, and an administrative and financial office in downtown Rio. Three different facilities, all separated, did not help business function smoothly.

Then one day we made a significant investment in Brazil. We located a 350,000-square-foot plant that had just been built and never put into operation. We consolidated the offices and plant, and all of a sudden we had a strong presence. We attracted good salesmen, marketing and manufacturing people, plus support staff, and the operation took off. It was worth it; our Brazilian company has been an excellent performer ever since, even though Brazilian economic policies have adversely affected us from time to time.

In the future I think it is going to be the multinationals that perform better than any other type of company. Of course there will be local enterprises springing up. But among the large and mature companies, it is the multinationals that will thrive, that can withstand all manner of foreign competition. Being multinational, having the business spread across the globe, is much like being diversified in the products you sell. It puts that many more threads in the company fabric.

ENTREPRENEURING IN LARGE ORGANIZATIONS

*"New ideas rarely proceed along foreseeable paths;
they need constant reevaluation and change."*

Success in innovation has long been one of the most important attributes of an effective large corporation. The innovation pioneers—AT&T, Du Pont, GE, and others—realized as early as 1900 that innovation could be managed strategically like any other aspect of the business. However, many of our large corporations are still trying to figure out how to do it. Over the years factions in the pioneering companies have waged battles over the appropriate roles for R & D labs, the relative importance of market focus versus basic technology research, and similar issues. These questions continue to occupy strategic planners today.

In most large companies a management style has evolved that emphasizes control and is structured as a hierarchy or pyramid. This authoritarian style has been used in most companies for managing both production and innovation, although there is much talk of decentralization. Business schools are still training people in analytic techniques that lead to centralization, by allowing managers at the top to make abstract decisions based on a small amount of numerical information. This analytic, top-down style has turned out to be a poor way to manage innovation, and the Japanese are now discovering that it may not even be the best way to manage production.

Most innovations, even in large organizations, emerge from visionary, but practical people, whom Gifford Pinchot has labeled "intrapreneurs." These people function by responding both to the imperatives of new technology and the needs of the market. As individuals, they have a dual vision that most strategic planning groups have not been able to achieve.

Like entrepreneurs, intrapreneurs have the courage and the broad vision to carry their ideas all the way from conception to the marketplace. They have the skills to build an effective project team, to find sponsors or champions when they need them, to locate technical, financial, and other resources, and to have a clear, if ever-changing view of what the market is going to want and of how to supply it. They often have a kind of dedicated deviousness that makes them hide a project until it has reached such an advanced state of development that it is safe to let people know about it. Most of them refuse to be confined by the official descriptions of their jobs, crossing boundaries and working in other areas as the need arises.

Larry Don Moore from 3M is a perfect example of an intrapreneur. He was an inspired maintenance technician when he began to notice that many of the machines he was repairing had to be fixed over and over again for the same troubles. One of the worst was a machine that folded the jackets for computer floppy disks. He began to see ways that the folder could be made to work better, but was told that modifying machinery was not part of his job. Since he had the heart and soul of an intrapreneur, he started to remodel the machine anyway on his own time. His plant manager believed in him and protected him, even manipulating the system to get him the money he needed for his project. Moore had to keep the equipment operational while he was working on it, which slowed him down, but what he finally developed for 3M turned out to be the best folding equipment in the world. He has gone on to other equally exciting projects and is clearly a great asset to the company that was smart enough to grant him the freedom he needed to work, even though the work he did far exceeded the specifications of his job.

People like Moore do not flourish under strict management control. They often have the same kind of maverick personalities that we associate with entrepreneurs. They can be hard for managers to deal with. However, new ideas rarely proceed along foreseeable paths; they need constant reevaluation and change even in such fundamental areas as what market they will eventually supply. Intrapreneurs are quick to see when such changes are needed.

Chuck House's development of the moon-landing monitor is a good example of radical plan changing. Chuck and some of his Hewlett Packard colleagues had been working on a monitor that used oscilloscope and electronic lens technology for an FAA control tower monitor. The monitor that Chuck and his team developed made an important breakthrough in size reduction, but did not quite meet the FAA's specifications for resolution. Rather than viewing this apparent calamity as a failure, Chuck went out and did some personal market research for his product. He found a variety of new kinds of customers for it, but his own market research people gave him no support. Their research predicted that there would never be a market for more than thirty-two units. At this point, Dave Packard himself ordered the project cancelled, saying that he did not want to see it in the lab when he returned the next year.

With truly inspired deviousness, House accelerated the project so that it was already on the market, and therefore out of the lab, when Packard returned the next year. In its first year the monitor landed on the moon, was used in the first artificial heart transplant, and was part of a system for television special effects that won an Emmy. Annual sales reached $10 million and the product sold for ten years without a major design modification. In addition, its technology became a part of many subsequent Hewlett Packard products.

Intrapreneurs do not necessarily make good managers of mature businesses. They are normally not excited by the standard rewards that motivate managers, such as steps up the ladder and corner offices. What they want is the freedom of time, resources, and capital to get on with their current and future projects. Larry Don Moore summed up the intrapreneurial attitude when he said, "I'd rather get stuff done than have people brag on me." Intrapreneurs need managers for their functional expertise and for protection and help in boundary crossing, but they need very little day-to-day direction.

In 1985, Johnson Wax initiated a series of steps to encourage entrepreneurism among employees at all levels. At a seminar for management people, the company invited Gifford Pinchot III, author of Intrapreneuring, *to discuss innovation barriers in the corporate structure. Talking with Pinchot (right) are Sam Johnson and Ray Farley.*

In the late 1960s and early 1970s, executives at Du Pont, 3M, W. R. Grace, and a few other pioneering companies realized that innovation might proceed faster if it had an organization of its own. With this in mind they created new venture groups to seek out and help promising new businesses. By the mid 1970s, between a quarter and a third of *Fortune* 500 companies were trying them. Despite their popularity, however, most of the groups died within five years of their births, drowned in a sea of red ink. A large part of the reason for their failure was that they were managed in the same top-down way as the rest of the company. Innovation, it turned out, could not be directed, but had to be reacted to in an opportunistic way.

Today the need for innovation is greater than ever. The Third World has made it their business to make anything cheaper than we can. We are on an innovation treadmill. We have to innovate faster and faster just to stay where we are. The companies who meet this challenge to innovate will be the ones who develop ways of managing that allow intrapreneurs the freedom they need, so that they do not find it necessary to leave the company to start businesses of their own.

Johnson Wax is well along the road to becoming one of the new style of companies that effectively maximizes the talents of its intrapreneurs. A clear message has been sent to managers, telling them that sponsoring innovation is a major part of their job. We have instituted new reward and recognition systems to stimulate innovation and are working on more appropriate control systems.

The result of the 1935 expedition to Brazil was the formation of a company in Fortaleza which improved the development of the carnauba palm and modernized harvesting and processing.

*The members of the 1935 Johnson Carnauba Expedition to northeast Brazil were, from left,
J. A. Hoy, co-pilot and radio operator; E. H. Schlanser, pilot; H. F. Johnson Jr., President; R. P.
Gardiner, Purchasing Agent; and Dr. J.V. Steinle, Research Director.*

*The pioneering expedition that H. F. Johnson led to Brazil in 1935 was made in this giant Sikorsky
amphibian. His exploration for the carnauba palm led to the development of a new business.*

Some examples of intrapreneurship which were funded by the company's Intrapreneurial Seed Fund Committee include the development of a home cleaning service, a mail order catalog business for old familiar brands of Johnson products no longer in volume production, and the development of a fly line cleaner/conditioner for fly-fishing enthusiasts. All the individuals or task forces involved worked on market considerations, pricing, contracts, market testing, and customer and consumer relations. Within a year one of these, the mail order business, already was making a profit, and the fly-fishing product had been licensed to a distributor for his label.

With today's rate of change there is a greater need than ever before for independent activity in corporations. There simply is not time for new ideas to grind their way through complex layers of approval. Business schools have a critical role to play in training tomorrow's managers. These young men and women will have to help their corporations adjust the need for top-down or consensus management with their intrapreneurs' need to do their jobs in their own ways. Managers will have to learn to trust their people and allow them to be accountable for their own performance. They will have to learn how to be sponsors, for almost every successful intrapreneuer has sponsors who help him and protect him, often at the risk of their own careers. Tomorrow's executives will have to develop reward systems that are meaningful to their intrapreneurs and which create motivation for innovating. Above all, business schools should teach the techniques of entrepreneuring so that their graduates will be intrapreneurs or will know how to manage them for the benefit of their companies.

The young managers who are entering corporations today have goals and attitudes that should make it easy for them to adapt to new styles of management. They want to select their own jobs and they expect to be accountable for their own performance. More and more, innovators say that they want to succeed or fail with the fate of their projects. These young people do not respect authority or value job security as much as previous generations. What they want is the opportunity to pursue their dreams. They probably will not expect to exert as much control over their subordinates as their predecessors did. It is the executives of today that will have the hardest time adapting to their corporations' new needs. They will have to fight attitudes that have been successful in the past, and they will have to accept risks at a time in their careers when it is frightening to do so. They will have to substitute trust for complex controls and flexibility for rigid analysis. The executives at Johnson Wax welcome this challenge and look forward to a bright and innovative future.

PUBLIC RELATIONS—FAR MORE THAN MOST APPRECIATE

"Lack of identity can be just as fatal to an organization's success as it is to the success of an individual."

To survive as a credible, independent company, a top priority in every large firm should be its public relations. I believe this strongly because what people think about a business and its people, products, and practices shapes the public perception of a firm's personality. And if we agree that what people think affects their actions and is therefore important to a firm's success, then we want those impressions to be favorable. Indeed, public relations and public affairs departments are an important part of virtually all American businesses. Staffed with skilled professionals, these departments help top management communicate with a company's own employees, the local community, the media, and government. However an individual P.R. operation is organized, it is a vital communications link between a company and its many publics.

Public relations professionals help a corporation form and articulate information that the business needs to communicate. They provide the means of communicating views of good performance to others, and they advise top management on the right thing to do when faced with a public relations dilemma.

In my view, a company's public relations begins at the top with its chief executive. In this age of "corporate accountability" and public interest in such dealings, even at privately held firms business leaders must be open and treat public relations with the same care given financial statements.

My favorite definition of public relations is that it is the management function designed to increase profits directly or indirectly by *earning* public goodwill, through the communication of corporate accomplishments and policies in the public interest. A company defines itself by what it does and how it communicates with others. Lack of identity can be just as fatal to an organization's success as it is to the success of an individual.

Public relations starts with and revolves around the chief executive and his or her values. If he shows dedication to excellence and integrity and regard for human dignity, then other employees will take their lead from his approach.

As my father said at the First International Conference in 1957, "We do not think of public relations as a cloak which we can put on or take off at will. We have public relations regardless of whether or not we have a formalized program. Every member of this company, regardless of the job he or she fills, plays a role in our public relations, in what the public thinks of us, our personnel, and our products. We strive to have anything we do—whether it is a television program, a building, or a package design—reflect qualities of good taste and imagination."

This is, of course, public relations at its most basic level. As statistician and economist Elmo Roper once said, "The public passes judgment on business in three ways: as a maker of products, as a

This excerpt from a profit sharing speech made by H. F. Johnson Sr., son of the founder of Johnson Wax, on Christmas Eve, 1927, sets forth the truths upon which this company's approach to business has been built.

The Rest Is Shadow

When all is said and done
this business is nothing but a symbol
and when we translate this we find
that it means a great many people
think well of its products and that
a great multitude has faith in the integrity
of the men who make this product.

In a very short time
the machines that are now so lively
will soon become obsolete
and the big buildings for all their solidity
must some day be replaced.

But a business which symbolizes
can live so long as there are human beings alive,
for it is not built of such flimsy materials
as steel and concrete,
it is built of human opinions
which may be made to live forever.

The goodwill of the people
is the only enduring thing in any business.

It is the sole substance...

The rest is shadow!

neighbor, and as a corporate citizen of the U.S." Roper might well have added that companies also are judged as employers. In our case, Samuel Curtis Johnson, the company's founder, was a man of unquestioned integrity and high moral character. As a businessman, neighbor, and corporate citizen of his community, he earned the regard of all who knew him. So from a public relations standpoint, this company was off to a good start. A solid foundation was laid for the growth of the business and for winning the esteem of the public. From the time he started making products, he took care of his employees and tried to be a solid part of the community in which he operated. He inevitably generated public goodwill.

Earning goodwill is, to be sure, a management function that directly or indirectly can lead to increased profits. By continually communicating to the public word of the firm's good products, accomplishments, contributions to humanitarian and artistic projects, and so on, the company is enhancing its reputation. It is, certainly, tooting one's own horn. But this is necessary for establishing a firm's identity, which in turn can encourage prosperity and ensure survival.

Public relations is much more complicated for a large corporation today. Audiences are no longer only local. A well-managed company can also have a tremendous positive impact by making connections between countries through trade, technology transfer, and the exchange of people. Johnson Wax, through its many products, is part of every community in the United States and many others worldwide. It has thousands of employees—individual representatives of the firm—around the globe, dealing with all manner of communities, customers, and governments.

However, to obtain the public relations benefit of these far-flung activities one needs an organized effort. When a company enters the international arena—or even if it is just large in the U.S.—it must actively be concerned with public relations. A company cannot for long maintain good public relations merely as a producer and seller of products.

On the other hand, a company cannot simply do good deeds and wait for the public to pay attention. If the company doesn't call attention to its better achievements and more honorable endeavors, then it is not doing itself justice. There have been some very private people and corporations, for example, who have done good deeds but would say nothing in public about them. And these individuals and firms were not well regarded, although if the good works were known, their image certainly would have been different.

It is a plain fact that bad news grabs the most attention. Occasionally, though, good works make news. But a company has got to come up

The Johnson's Wax Pavilion at the New York World's Fair in 1964-65 was the hit of the fair; people lined up for hours at the Golden Rondelle Theater to see "To Be Alive!"

with something special to garner widespread attention. For instance, our Frank Lloyd Wright buildings and New York World's Fair exhibit were spectacular achievements that received much press and public attention because we dared to be different.

It has also been shown that positive results can come about by doing what one sees as the right thing to do in a seemingly bad situation.

For example, when concerns first appeared about the damage chlorofluorocarbons (CFC's) could cause to the atmosphere, we made an immediate decision to ban them from our products. But we also made sure the public at large knew of this move. We took this step in the interest of our customers, and we became known as the innovator and initiator of the movement away from chlorofluorocarbons.

So, good news in whatever form has to be fairly spectacular to draw widespread and long-term media and public attention. If the achievement is unique, creative, and distinctive, then it can't help but get exposure through the media. But few companies seem to understand that point, including some that are otherwise fine firms.

Studying a model of the Johnson Wax Pavilion, designed by Lippincott & Margulies, Inc., were, from left, Howard M. Packard, then President, Robert Moses, fair president, and H. F. Johnson, then Chairman of the company.

The magazine *Business and Society* once asked 215 individuals and groups involved in consumerism activities to compare corporations according to their "social responsiveness and accountability to the public interest." Ranked at the top of the list was Johnson Wax—ahead of Procter & Gamble, Lever, and Colgate. In 1984, we were ranked among the "100 best companies to work for in America" in the book *The 100 Best Companies to Work for in America*, by Robert Levering, Milton Moskowitz, and Michael Katz. We like to think that various P.R. activities carried out over the years contributed to these top rankings.

Our approach to public relations is not unlike the Product Plus theory. That "plus" in corporate activities is just as important to a corporation's public image as it is to a new consumer product. People have higher expectations of corporations than most executives believe. People expect companies to give to the United Fund in the normal course of business. They have come to expect executives to be good people in the community. They expect local companies not to dump junk into the river behind the plant. Therefore, if a chief executive does all these routine things, which may sound like more than enough good practices, he still has met only the public's basic expectations.

In the book *In Search of Excellence*, Tom Peters and Bob Waterman argue that "Excellent companies tend to be companies where employees are proud of the place where they work." Part of this pride is in the firm's reputation of being above the thundering herd of most other companies. The practical result of this pride is that the company is able to hire better people than are drawn into the herd. Potential employees sense the degree of excellence in a corporation. And good public relations—all forms of public relations—helps project that excellence.

In his latest book, *A Passion for Excellence*, written with Nancy Austin, Peters says:

> S. C. Johnson & Son (Johnson Wax, etc.), the superb Racine, Wisconsin, company, joins the list of the bold. Late in 1984, Chairman Sam Johnson observed that his British subsidiary apparently felt estranged from the Johnson "family feeling" he so cherishes. To rectify the situation, he chartered a 747 and flew all five hundred employees of the British subsidiary to the United States for a full week. Three days were spent touring U.S. factories and attending a lavish gala in Racine put on by the U.S. work force; two more days were devoted to sightseeing in New York City.

We did it all over again in 1987 when we invited the entire Australian company and its retirees to visit headquarters on their 70th Anniversary. In appreciation for what they told us was "a trip of a

On the occasion of their 70th anniversaries, British Johnson in 1984 and Australian Johnson in 1987 visited Racine. In both cases the whole company was invited to meet with counterparts in the U.S. and to visit at the homes of Racine employees.

lifetime," the 230 Australian employees and retirees left behind at the Racine Zoo as a gift to the community six kangaroos and six wallaroos which had flown over with them, with many of the marsupials ready to bear young!

Another example comes to mind. When we invite a talented young person to Racine, an individual practically any corporation would be delighted to hire, we take him—or her—through the Wax Company, the Frank Lloyd Wright buildings. We soon notice this person looking up, around the columns, and then observing the prospect as he goes up in the round elevators. We can almost hear him thinking: "You know, there is something special about this company." And a creative person, who considers himself special, will feel he has something to give to such a company. Most good people think they have something extra to offer to the world, and don't want to waste it on just any old company. They want to be appreciated and have their abilities used to the fullest.

Excellent companies attract excellent people, which in turn perpetuates the cycle. And we feel our company's concern for excellence is obvious to anyone who visits Racine. In fact, the image extends far beyond headquarters.

One cannot simply go into a "P.R. mode" when it seems appropriate. As in other areas of activity, we must act from a set of policies and principles. We must keep the public relations aspects of everything we do in mind, and it is vitally important that our efforts include an open relationship with the news media, which still are among the most active arenas for public relations.

We grant that television tends to be a superficial medium. The national evening news is like a headline service, and many local stations are more likely to focus on events which are spectacular than on stories of substance. So be it. Millions of Americans rely on television almost exclusively for their news. Businessmen must live with this fact and adapt to TV's limitations.

Print reporters operate under severe deadline pressure, and many of the mistakes they make are due to the speed at which they must gather and write their reports. Moreover, the spoken word is often imprecise; the reporter may jot down what he is told, but the speaker may not have done a thorough job of articulating what he *meant*. What I am saying is that business people who *think* they are "misquoted" may be as much at fault for a mistake as the reporter.

So, what does one do? Well, a good public relations effort includes educating the press, and I don't mean that in a derogatory way. For instance, during the Arab oil embargo in the early 1970s, the media ripped apart the American petroleum industry. Reporters actually broadcast and wrote about rumors of tankers waiting off the U.S. coast for the price to rise. Few writers and broadcasters had the slightest idea of how the oil industry worked. Prior to 1973, they really had no reason to learn.

However, before the oil industry could get a fair shake in the press, petroleum P.R. people had to do a lot of explaining of how that complicated business worked. Companies had to admit when they made mistakes, talk frankly about the squeeze put on the nation by OPEC and by a shortage of oil, and have the patience to explain the ins and outs of the oil business in layman's terms. Now, to a large degree, oil companies have relations with the press as good as any other business.

At Johnson Wax, we have adopted a series of hints on how to deal with the media. These are not a panacea, but simple precepts that serve our people as a guide. They are as follows:

1. Don't refuse an interview with a legitimate and professional member of the press. When called, say you will return the call when free, and have the public relations staff check the caller's credentials, affiliation, and authenticity.

2. Avoid saying "no comment" since this could be interpreted as a tacit agreement or an admission of guilt. The media, if thwarted, will undoubtedly try to obtain news from less informed, and possibly less friendly, sources.

3. If you don't know the answer, don't speculate! Say you will get the information and call back as soon as possible—and keep your promise! Buy yourself the time you need, but also try to honor the reporter's

deadline.

4. Provide the media with relevant business news, both good and bad, but avoid divulging business strategies that might help the competition or involve private matters. Avoid discussion of any pending or likely deals, acquisitions, exclusive licensing arrangements, et cetera, until cleared with the other party.

5. Be very careful not to say anything disparaging about another person or company. Be alert to controversial or negative statements or questions set as a trap to invite your comment.

6. Do not accept offers to speak "off the record"! Do not say or write anything that you would not want to see quoted or broadcast.

7. Get legal advice in advance (and, if possible, in writing) from the Law Department, if the reporter's questions involve litigation, whether present or future, and whether internal or external in terms of the company and its employees.

8. Take the initiative when important bad news is to be publicized. Tell as much as you can, since this type of candor and honesty defuses the issue.

9. Do your homework. Draft a news release or prepare for an interview with the help of the public relations staff and other relevant

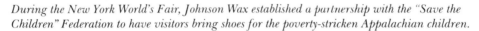

During the New York World's Fair, Johnson Wax established a partnership with the "Save the Children" Federation to have visitors bring shoes for the poverty-stricken Appalachian children.

executives whenever a story is about to break, either good or bad. Anticipate questions and prepare appropriate answers that are complete and well thought-through.

10. In the event of *minor* errors of fact, do not ask for retractions or try to rebut allegations—this will only fan the fire. Challenge *major* errors, but respect the reporter's authority and appeal to the reporter for a correction before going over his or her head.

11. As a defense against misquotes it is advisable to keep a record of all telephone interviews. For all media inquiries it is essential to write down the reporter's name, organization, phone number, time, date, and circumstances leading up to the call.

12. Take actions that are obviously in the public interest, with no apparent profit motive, and inform the media. Make yourself available to represent the company's viewpoint on these activities.

13. Maintain a positive attitude toward the media. Assume that they are trying to do their job professionally. Know your reporters and editors, accommodate them, inform them.

Of course, when yours is a large company in a relatively small town, you must take care not to dominate the local media. This is a delicate balance. You don't want to be secretive, but you also don't want to be in print or on television every day. So we try to get out the good news about the company at appropriate times, and if the news is used, fine. If it isn't, we don't complain but merely let the good works stand on their own.

Public relations starts with a firm's reputation with its employees and with other citizens of its community, extends outward with good products advertised honestly and innovative and charitable projects, and is further advanced by a good working relationship with the media. In return, a company draws both excellent talent to work for it and the respect of consumers. The function is carried out not only by skilled public relations professionals, but by company executives, truck drivers, and salesmen—in short, by everyone at the firm. One might say that public relations is a very fundamental business in any company.

EMPLOYEE RELATIONS— OUR PEOPLE MAKE IT GO

"Part of our secret for success: the pride of everyone working in a company that has a set of principles that transcends the generations."

One of the threads that weaves through the immensely popular and insightful book, *In Search of Excellence*, concerns the degree to which "excellent" companies motivate their employees. Excellent firms, the authors found, encourage an entrepreneurial spirit even in large settings, but many other large companies have lost this spirit somewhere along the way.

I think this is an accurate observation. What worries me most about public relations and employee relations and other staff operations is that as we get bigger in the United States, and all over the world, we might tend to develop a bureaucracy of our own. The bigger a company gets, the greater the tendency is to develop a bureaucratic middle layer. It concerns me that this middle layer might get in the way of appropriate communications between the creative level, which typically exists below the bureaucracy, and top management, where decisions are made to take initiatives that can move a company in more entrepreneurial directions.

The average Johnson person is quite knowledgeable about what we do, and we are sensitive to individual attitudes. We want our employees to be proud of working here. That's part of the secret of our success: the pride of everyone in working for a company that has a set of principles which transcends the generations.

Our basic philosophy is to push decisions down to the lowest competent level. I don't want any more decisions in the chairman's office than I have to make: there are plenty of people at other levels in the company who can make most of the decisions. This policy helps develop the decision-making ability of individuals at all ranks.

This is probably one of the principal challenges for the next generation. We need to be careful about the balance between the creative level and the bureaucratic level. We never want to have too

Hand-filled cans were hand packed one hundred to a handmade wooden box and hand trucked to the shipping room, where they were handloaded into horse-drawn drays. The wagons took the load to the Racine dock to be shipped by water. The year is 1911.

many levels of management and too many "in betweens"; we would never want a good idea from an employee in New Zealand to be stalled somewhere and not be available for use on a global basis.

I think another common thread throughout those companies called "Excellent" is that they allow good ideas to move up or down to the appropriate level where they can be acted on. The message, therefore, for the chief executive and his team is continually to work on keeping those communications channels open and ideas moving in the proper direction.

The authors of *In Search Of Excellence* talk about management by "walking around." I like that phrase. What it really means is that top management is available. The authors cite the example of David Packard, who practices management by walking around. He visits people in their offices and in the factories. It is a good idea, and it makes me feel slightly guilty that I don't get around as much as I used to. Walking around can give you new perspectives on what employees are doing; maybe the chief executive can even make a helpful suggestion.

Back in 1933 we had limited product categories—floor care, auto care, and furniture care—with accessory products to apply, buff, or polish surfaces. S. C. Johnson and Son consisted of my father and four vice presidents, the management, and about 350 other people. That was the wax works, the whole company. They all could communicate with each other very nicely. Because of the scope of the company's operations today, we need different forms of communication than

The office force in 1910 was comprised of all women, except for the office "boy" perched in the tree.

The first meeting of the Twenty Year Club was held on January 13, 1937 with twenty-seven members. Today, the huge JMBA Recreation and Fitness Center gym can barely accommodate the number of members attending the annual meeting; some 780 participate from a membership that exceeds 1,300.

were required by that small team. But my father and his colleagues established some of the basics which still serve as the foundation for good employee relations.

The one idea in the Peters and Waterman book with which I probably disagree the most is the conclusion that companies which have focused on one field, or have "stuck to their knitting" as they say, have done the best. I think we have "multiple visions," and that we have succeeded because of that. The authors and I had a bit of an argument about this. I think we are an exception to the rule. I see multiple visions of the future for our firm. After all, we have succeeded in many businesses, from financial services to specialty chemicals.

In "This We Believe," our corporate philosophy, we state that people are our most important resource. We believe in treating people with dignity. The results of this philosophy are seen in the employee benefits which have been initiated over the years, starting with paid vacations in 1900 and both profit sharing and group life insurance as well as the eight-hour work day in 1917. Throughout the years we have added the forty-hour work week (1926), a pension plan (1934), hospitalization coverage (1939), the Lighthouse Resort (1951), deferred profit sharing and major medical insurance (1953), Armstrong Park (1957), dental care coverage (1975), vision care (1978), the JMBA Recreation Center (1980), a Child Care Center (1985), and an Aquatic Center (1987).

We believe that anyone at any level can have a good idea and that everyone ought to be able to talk with anyone else in the firm. It is better to err on the side of more communications rather than less. It is important to recognize people for their achievements and to respect them as individuals. We are also growth oriented. I don't know how to run a company that doesn't give people new mountains to climb.

We believe in teamwork and discourage company politics of a destructive kind. We also try to suppress status differences, particularly by reducing those differences which divide management and labor in most companies. Many years ago we did away with time clocks in the factory to help eliminate factory-employee versus office-employee differences, for example.

In our company, at least, I don't believe there is a distinction between management and labor; we are all Johnson people. We all have a great deal of interest in this business; we all sit on one side of the table. We all share in the pretax profits. As far as I can tell, the parking lot is the only place where status is evident; I simply haven't solved that one yet. Incidentally, most universities haven't figured that one out either. We never could solve it at Cornell. It is still one of the thorniest issues the faculty argues about.

The JMBA Aquatic Center opened in fall of 1987 and features an L-shaped swimming pool with six 25-yard lanes and six 25-meter lanes. Other features include a children's pool, a whirlpool, a fitness room, and an aerobics room.

Lighthouse Resort in northern Wisconsin was established for employees in 1951. The resort provides a wide variety of fun and relaxing activities for employees and dependents while they live in completely furnished and equipped cottages at a minimal weekly rate.

The globe (above) was a surprise gift to Sam Johnson from U.S. employees.

Johnson Wax has had only one or two unions in any of its plants, here in the United States or around the world. The word "union" is not used in our "This We Believe" statement. Our practice is to create the kind of working environment in which employees do not feel it is necessary to get a third party to assist them in their relationship with management. To maintain this kind of environment, we encourage bottom-up communications in five ways.

First, we work very hard to make the normal relationship between employee and supervisor mutually rewarding and communicative, so that employees feel free to talk about any kind of on- or off-the-job problem. Second, if an employee doesn't get satisfaction from a supervisor, he or she can then go above the supervisor and talk to the boss's boss without fear of recrimination. That can continue upward, even to my office.

Third, we encourage our personnel department and its people to be yet another conduit of upward communication. Many of the most common problems have to do with personnel matters: paid benefits, vacations, working conditions, promotion opportunities, and so forth.

The people in the personnel department act in some ways as a substitute for union stewards.

Fourth, we maintain a special line of communications called "Just Ask." Through this program, which has been running for more than fifteen years, we encourage employees to submit questions to a confidential source. The source then seeks answers from the appropriate person, without identifying the employee who asked the question. Many employees don't want to bother personnel or their bosses, but do want an answer to their questions. In addition to answering the employees directly, "Just Ask" routes the answers— without the names—to all of the supervisors so that they know what kinds of questions the employees are asking and what the responses are.

And our fifth upwards-communications vehicle is our employee opinion surveys which we take every two or three years. The most important aspect of this program is that all segments of the company develop action plans to address issues raised by the surveys.

We have worked hard at eliminating dividing lines. That is why a union does not fit into our picture. Unions seek to emphasize divisions between management and those they seek to organize. Sometimes a dividing line is a false one that doesn't make a lot of sense, particularly if you have quite a bit of mobility among groups and people are able to move up the line. Profit sharing, and the other benefits and programs I have described which extend throughout the company, tend to erase that dividing line.

It may be that our central vision is how we select, motivate, train, and organize our people for action in whatever business field we are trying to compete. After all, our basic strength lies in the people who work here, and this strength has its source not only in their talents, but in the attitudes they have toward the company and their work. This is the strength that will carry us successfully into new ventures.

Our corporate culture fosters a creative environment in which communication and participation are encouraged in all decisions appropriate to one's level. It is a culture of security because we have no layoffs for economic fluctuations. It is a culture that identifies with the family and with the traditions of the family, both the Johnson family and the many other families whose members work here. It is a culture in which employees are seldom fired. We do fire people, but the perception is that we are very hesitant to do so. If somebody has to be fired, I consider it our mistake. Either we put the person in the wrong job, we did not manage him appropriately, we promoted him to his level of incompetence, or we hired the wrong person in the first place.

There have been occasions, because of mismanagement or a

Armstrong Park was opened in 1957 and houses not only the JMBA center with its fitness and wellness program, but a new indoor acquatics center as well. Besides being the site for most company functions, such as the annual picnic, it is popular for family outings and parties.

changed competitive environment, for example, when we have found it necessary to sell or restructure a troubled operation. People have been encouraged to retire early, encouraged to take retraining if alternative positions are available, or have been released to accomplish a permanent reduction of staff in order to keep the operation competitive. This has not happened very often, and we try to manage the company so that it won't happen; but when it does, our commitment is to act in a sensitive and helpful manner.

We also have a continuity of management in the Johnson family that means we don't have a CEO coming in every six years to do his own thing in his own way. There is a continuity of culture and of philosophy that bridges the generations. The concept of profit sharing is probably the central idea to our philosophy of employee relations. It represents a reward for participation in the company's success; it shows that people have a stake in the ownership. Profit sharing symbolizes our approach to management.

SERVICE TO OTHERS THROUGH VOLUNTEER ACTION

"People can get excited about volunteering. It has a two-way benefit—a benefit to the community or organization and a benefit to the person and his company."

There is a greater degree of volunteer activity in the United States than in almost any other place in the world. In fact, it is estimated that four out of ten Americans regularly perform volunteer service valued at $67 billion in donated time. Volunteers are called the "glue" of American society. I have lived in England and have traveled extensively, and from my observations I have come to believe that while people in other countries volunteer during crises, day-to-day volunteer action is neither as intense nor as extensive as it is in the United States.

I think that in Europe and in other countries there is a greater expectation on the part of the public that the government will provide much of what we in the United States would rather do ourselves as individuals. Our tradition, which is challenged from time to time, is to help others, rather than to allow government to get bigger in order to take on these tasks.

The spirit of volunteer service and action is not new. Back in the 1830s, the French writer Alexis de Tocqueville reported after his visit to the U.S. that the health of a democratic society can be measured by the functions performed by its private citizens on their own initiative.

We at Johnson Wax sometimes must persuade our overseas managers that it is appropriate to be a volunteer or to donate money to a worthy local cause. This is because there is not a tradition of voluntarism or charitable works in most of the countries in which we do business.

We had an interesting experience in Cyprus. Our operation there is relatively new, and we employ Lebanese, Moroccans, and members of several other nationalities. The team there decided they should do something in the area of voluntarism or charity since it was an objective of the parent company. Well, they really did a spectacular first effort!

They learned that a new wing was needed on a hospital for mentally retarded children. Because of a lack of space the hospital could only retain children up to age twelve, even if they needed additional training and help. The new wing was to house older children and permit them to stay longer for necessary training.

So Johnson in Cyprus gave money for the new wing and even helped plan the facility itself. I was invited to dedicate it. At the dedication were the President and Vice President of Cyprus, the Archbishop of the Greek Orthodox Church, and half the Assembly of the national government. They thought we had done the greatest thing in the whole world and wanted us to know how they felt. No other company had ever done anything of this kind before. They were astounded that a corporation would do something to meet a genuine need in the community without expecting something in return.

All our Cyprus employees were there—all twenty-seven of them— and they received something out of the experience, too. They grew in their sense of themselves, from people working for just an ordinary company to people who were proud of their association with the place where they worked.

That is part of the greatness of voluntarism—mutual benefit that results from enlightened self interest. For example, nearly every city and town in the United States has a United Way, which is the focal point of volunteer agencies and volunteer activity. My grandfather was one of the founders of the united community fund idea in Racine, which was formed to bring volunteer agencies together so they could more effectively raise the money they needed to fulfill their purposes. Before this united campaign concept, fund raising was fragmented and people were approached almost daily to give financial support to a wide variety of agencies.

But raising money is only one part of voluntarism; indeed, it is not the most important. A more important part is the devotion of time by the people who actually serve the organizations and spend a good portion of their free time working at no pay.

I think we are happily and uniquely endowed in this country with volunteer spirit. And I don't see any diminution of this enthusiasm, either. In fact, I think that as our population ages there will be even more people available and willing to do volunteer work than ever before. In Racine we see many retired people working hard as volunteers—sometimes giving more time than they ever could when they were employed.

An effort in Racine to revitalize the whole downtown is and has

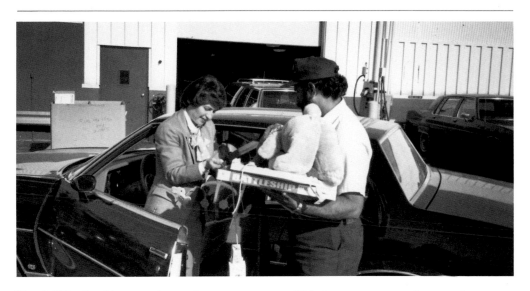

"People Who Care" is an employee volunteer program established to encourage employees to share some of their time and talents in worthwhile projects, such as spearheading a toy collection at Christmas through the community's Toys for Tots program.

been largely a volunteer effort. A grassroots campaign was successfully engineered to build a festival site, and the community and the private sector got together on several major development efforts. We participated in setting up an organization called the Downtown Racine Development Corporation, and they had no trouble whatsoever in gaining enthusiastic volunteers to participate and contribute not only their money but their time.

The downtown effort is making real headway. Our county government committed millions to develop the harbor for recreational use, the city government facilitated the development of a festival site, and private donations from both corporations and many individuals built a Festival Hall. The project has been an outstanding melding of private volunteers, private money, public funds, and community cooperation. It is one of the first times I can remember when the county and the city, businesses, the downtown merchants group, and individual citizens have all committed themselves to a common goal. It has been an exhilarating experience, but not unique to Racine or to Wisconsin. This concept is beginning to develop around the world.

People can get excited about volunteering. It has a two-way benefit— a benefit to the community or organization and a benefit to the person and his company. I find it hard to believe that other companies will not even consider this double benefit. But many companies do not foster voluntarism. They think it takes away from a person's time on the job, or that it detracts from the tasks at hand when they do something that

The "Grand Old Man" of Racine, S. C. Johnson, laid the cornerstone for the YMCA Building on June 26, 1915. He had deep community convictions and unbounded generosity, legacies he left to future generations.

Begun in 1981 and named for the late Chairman Emeritus Herbert F. Johnson, Jr., the Community Service Award recognizes U.S. employees and retirees who are making valuable contributions to society through their involvement in community services. The award is $5,000 in contributions in the winner's name to selected charities.

is peripheral to the mainstream of the business. That is absolutely not true. A good executive, a busy executive, always has time to do some other things, especially for the good of the community.

My father believed that we couldn't have a healthy environment inside the company unless we had a healthy environment outside in the community. We wouldn't be able to hire good people for the company, for example, unless there was a good community for them to live in.

This "Inside/Out" or "Outside/In" theory holds water, I think. And seeing a company's concern for its outside environment inspires employees and others to pitch in and do their share in maintaining the quality of life in the community. If business owners just took it upon themselves in voluntary and constructive ways to help improve the ten blocks around their places of business, we might cure a good-sized portion of the urban blight that exists in this country.

For voluntarism to take hold as part of a company's culture, there must be a key executive who sets the example by personal involvement. A family-owned business, because of its roots and its flexibility, or a locally owned business because of its self-interest, has a much greater sense of the community and a greater sense of community responsibility than does a company whose headquarters is in a distant city.

Obviously, I know that volunteer activities can be overdone. Business people could spend all of their time in civic or social activities of a volunteer nature and ignore the operation of their companies, but that is an extreme that easily can be avoided.

I spend a good twenty to thirty percent of my time, or about two days of every seven, on what I call "not-for-profit" activities. These include such responsibilities as being Regent of the Smithsonian Institution and Chairman of The Johnson Foundation (which don't take much time), as well as serving as a trustee of Cornell University and as Chairman of the Board of Trustees of The Mayo Foundation, both of which take substantial time. But they are worth it! I learn a lot from these activities.

My exposure to the Mayo Foundation over the past fifteen years or so has given me an understanding of the health care field that I never would have gotten any other way. This experience may in time help our business, since we are beginning to move into the health care field.

At Johnson Wax, the business of business has always been to do more than simply meet the needs of our customers, our employees, and our shareholders. Although these responsibilities will always exist and are vitally important, we also realized early that we had an obligation to the communities in which we operate. We have found over the years that we have made a difference to them and will continue to support the local voluntarism which is our vehicle for making a difference.

The central focus of voluntarism for Johnson has been and is *people*—people involved in their communities by teaching, counseling, advocating legislation, serving on agency boards, and, when necessary and appropriate, using the resources of the corporation for the betterment of local conditions. According to a recent Gallup poll, some 85 million Americans, more than one-half the adult population, donate some part of their time as volunteers. I have long felt that this kind of spirit—a spirit that surmounts selfishness—deserves encouragement and recognition wherever and whenever possible.

When we adopted our corporate philosophy statement, "This We Believe," in 1976, we made service to one's community an important foundation of the document. To show support for that principle, we established a "This We Believe" Award to honor those Johnson companies worldwide which demonstrate significant achievements in community involvement. Considerable competition has developed around the world to win the award.

Several years ago, to encourage continuing volunteer service to others, our company established the H. F. Johnson Community Service Award. This award recognizes our U.S. employees, who, on their own and without pay or company sponsorship, have made valuable contributions through volunteer service to improve the quality of life in their communities. The winner gets to name his or her favorite charity or charities to receive $5,000, and the employee receives a Steuben crystal to commemorate the occasion. Up to five runners-up can be selected who get to name a charity of their choice for a $500 contribution. We have a parallel program for retirees which offers the same awards.

My father, for whom the award was named, always encouraged our people to involve themselves in social, cultural, and educational projects which enhance the quality of life. He was himself active in many community service projects.

My father passed on the heritage of voluntarism to me, and I have been grateful for the inheritance. I cannot understand how people run businesses without being part of their community. It is such an enriching part of the whole enterprise of being a professional businessman in America.

CORPORATE PHILANTHROPY AND SOCIAL RESPONSIBILITY

"At our company, corporate social responsibility can be redrafted to read 'corporate opportunity.'"

My great-grandfather, a true church-going man, believed in corporate philanthropy. He held the notion that businesses should put back something into the community in which they are located. By various extensions and indirect methods, a corporation also should give back something to the broader group of consumers from which it has earned profits. Providing jobs in a community, he believed, while certainly important, was simply not enough.

His concept is, of course, in the tradition of the Carnegie, Mellon, and Rockefeller families. And although Johnson Wax—then a little Midwestern parquet flooring manufacturer—could not be philanthropic on so grand a scale, my grandfather carried on his father's notion and set the tone for the company's tradition of giving "something" back. As founder of the United Fund, he even gave an endowment to the charity which is used to provide money for the volunteers' campaign luncheon and dinner report meetings. My grandfather did this simply so that no one could say his or her donation was used to entertain the volunteers.

My father gave away most of his money during his lifetime, to varied causes including Cornell University and The Johnson Foundation. The Johnson family has long believed that basically one should give money away as it is made, rather than passing funds along in an estate. After all, it is a lot more fun to give it away while you are alive than to have trustees do it after you are gone.

My father was very active in giving—a practice I have followed— right up to the maximum the Internal Revenue Service allows an individual to deduct. This has become something of a family tradition. Accumulated wealth really isn't very important. If it just sits there, what good does it do? Personal wealth should be reinvested in productive enterprises, just as a corporation does with part of its earnings, or it should be put to use in a philanthropic way. I find the thought of sitting on a pile of money, a passive investor in a portfolio of managed funds, utterly boring. To me, clipping coupons is not a very dynamic way to live.

Therefore, if one is a wealthy individual—to the point where he or she has provided for his family's security and children's education—he ought to invest in enterprises in which he has a hand. Or, invest in a philanthropic way, in institutions which are worthy and in which a donor might be able to have a hand as well. Philanthropy is part of an active person's involvement in the community and in the charities and causes one thinks are worthy.

The corporate philanthropic policies of Johnson Wax are not fundamentally different from those of the Johnson family. It was either my grandfather or father who started giving five percent of the company's pretax profits to charity. At the time it was the maximum deductible contribution allowed by the IRS. And that percentage now is built into the company's total cost structure: it is a way of life.

At our company, corporate social responsibility can be redrafted to read "corporate opportunity."

Our definition of corporate social responsibility is not to do only what is expected morally or required by law. Rather, it is to apply our corporate and personal talents and resources to make a significant difference in our communities. We are obligated to hold a broad perception of our own self-interest. Social responsibility recognizes that the health of our communities, our schools, our governments, bears on the health of the corporation. And, in turn, the health of the corporation bears on the well-being of its most important resource— its people.

There are really three ways to fulfill social responsibility.

First is the involvement of corporate employees in community activities, which I described earlier. Certainly, money is a necessity, but money alone cannot compensate for the kind of human expertise and compassion so many organizations depend upon from their volunteers.

Often business people can use their talents to help agencies operate more efficiently and effectively. And it has been my experience that community involvement can be equally beneficial to those who volunteer by exposing them to problems outside their normal areas of responsibility. At Johnson Wax we encourage and facilitate employee involvement.

The second major way is legislative and governmental involvement, not only on legislation that directly affects the company, but equally on the legislative needs of our cities, schools, the arts, the handicapped, and so on.

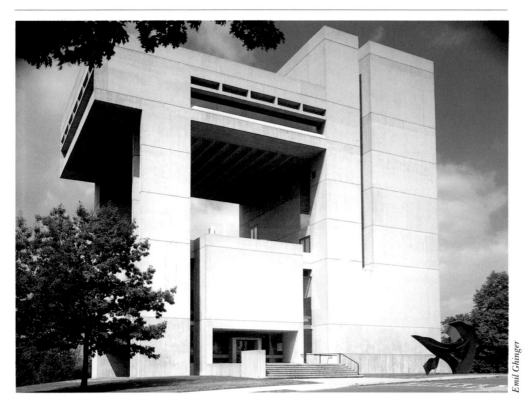

Emil Ghinger

Mr. Johnson is greeted warmly at the dedication of the H. F. Johnson Museum of Art at Cornell. Mr. Johnson gave a gift of $4.8 million that made the museum possible. I. M. Pei designed the concrete structure.

There are needs that require the payment of taxes, and it is important to approach those needs from a balanced viewpoint. We will not succeed in revitalizing our cities if we do not meet the reasonable needs of their citizens. We have an obligation to pay our share of taxes and to see that these reasonable needs are met.

And, finally, there are cash contributions. The concept of corporate giving is as old as the modern corporation itself. It is also a concept that has steadily increased with the rise of business income. In 1940, for example, when their income totaled $10 billion, corporations donated $38 million to non-profit organizations. Today U.S. corporate income has surpassed $223 billion, and non-profit organizations, ranging from public television to institutions such as the University of Wisconsin, share $4.4 billion in corporate donations.

Since World War II, there has been a precept within the corporate world that if you want to be seen as part of the responsible community, you should be contributing approximately one percent of your income. This one percent figure has almost become standard among

Sam Johnson assisted in the dedication of the Johnson Wing of the NEA Eleousa Home for the developmentally disabled in Cyprus. A major contribution from Cyprus Johnson enabled the home to build this special wing for adults.

major companies. You also hear a lot about the "Two Percent Club" in cities like Minneapolis and Chicago. Johnson Wax in the United States, as I mentioned, has been a member of the rare "Five Percenter Club."

There is and probably always will be a running debate about the merits of corporate philanthropy. There are those who oppose almost all corporate charity. Nobel-winning economist Milton Friedman is supposedly the headmaster of the give-nothing school. He has said, "This is a fundamentally subversive doctrine; the claim that business should contribute to the support of charitable activities is an inappropriate use of corporate funds in a free enterprise society."

But even Mr. Friedman makes exceptions. First, he says closely held corporations may contribute directly to charity "to lessen the tax bite." He also approves of contributions to local institutions, such as hospitals, colleges, museums and parks, *when* they provide marginal returns to the company. Our philosophy is hardly so self-centered.

There are many reasons corporations who have a social conscience make contributions. For example, two-thirds of all the private contributions to public television come from oil companies. Oil companies, particularly Mobil and Exxon, have really made public television their preserve. The reason is image making. Surveys have shown that having the Mobil name appear along with "Masterpiece Theatre" on public television, no matter how briefly, has a very favorable effect on the way people view Mobil.

Another reason for giving: companies are continually looking for ways to improve the morale of their employees and to recruit quality managers. Giving money to organizations that employees favor is considered good employee relations. Ninety percent of all corporate money, in fact, is awarded in the home region, partly because it will have a more visible impact on employees. Approximately half of all large companies also have matching gift programs which allow employees to define where the money will go by contributing an initial gift themselves.

Each year in the U.S., our philanthropic arm, The Johnson's Wax Fund, Inc., matches the individual contributions of employees to the United Ways in all the communities in which we have employees, some 270 throughout the land. It also matches contributions to high schools and colleges.

Another reason why money is given out locally is because in many companies, including ours, corporate culture dictates that business take part in community organizations. And one of our criteria is that we would favor a request that came from an organization in which our employees are actively involved and give of their own money.

In answer to some of the criticism leveled against corporate

The Johnson Foundation was established more than sixty years ago. Since 1960 it has had its headquarters at Wingspread, the former home of H. F. Johnson Jr. More than 1,000 educational conferences and 1,500 special events have been sponsored by the Foundation at Wingspread.

For the past decade, the Wax Fund has made contributions in support of a Red-crowned crane research and captive breeding program at the International Crane Foundation in Baraboo, WI. Additionally, Mr. & Mrs. S. C. Johnson personally made a grant for this crane housing pod at ICF.

contributions, I'd like to offer some viewpoints.

Most corporations conduct their social responsibility programs on an enlightened self-interest basis. For example, if your headquarters is located in a broken-down neighborhood, it is hard to hire good employees. Shouldn't companies try to improve the neighborhood so they can hire better people to enhance their profit performance? Isn't it appropriate for corporations to support the universities that they recruit from, because that helps assure the quality of their future management? Isn't it appropriate for corporations to support research at a university in an area that might have some technological importance to the corporation in the long run? Isn't it appropriate for corporations to support cultural and educational activities in their communities so that the quality of life is not only better for everyone, but especially their own employees?

In large corporations, charitable decisions are most always handled by a committee of responsible executives (and, at Johnson Wax, some lower-level people, too). These people live in their community, know their community, and understand the needs of the community. Isn't it better to have thousands of people in thousands of companies responding to identified needs in communities across the country, than it is to let all of those charitable decisions be made in Washington or in the State capitols by bureaucrats less responsive to the true needs of each community?

Not only do corporations involve themselves financially in their communities, but they almost universally supply people to assist local social agencies, sometimes on company time. This cannot be measured in dollars and cents.

Racine isn't our only "home." We are in other communities in the United States and in other cities all over the world. We encourage our general managers to follow the home company's lead, and insist that there is nothing inconsistent with having both a tightly run operation and a full-fledged philanthropic program.

Our companies worldwide support a wide variety of programs and projects, from buying motorized life rafts in Australia to funding a bookmobile that serves 250 provincial high schools in the Philippines. We have supported a community newspaper in Japan, a business college in France, and a major exposition on national architectural achievements in Belgium.

The company also is a major supporter of The Johnson Foundation, founded by my father, whose principal role is to be a convener of conferences related to education, the human environment, and international understanding. The gatherings are held at Wingspread, my father's home where I grew up, which has been converted into a conference center and headquarters for the Foundation. I feel privileged to serve as Chairman of an esteemed board of trustees dedicated to making Wingspread a place for decision makers and active people to meet and discuss the most important problems facing our global society. Maybe out of these conferences will come some solutions that will make a difference in our world.

Corporate philanthropy and corporate social responsibility are imprecise concepts: We are dealing with complex issues, emotions, people and cultures. The most creative ideas can fail. And money often is not the only solution. Still, by providing creative ideas, and both human and financial resources, we believe we can make a difference. Moreover, I know we have made a difference, simply by looking around at many of the communities in which we Johnson people live and work.

ARCHITECTURE—A TRADITION OF EXCELLENCE

". . . we want our buildings to convey our commitment of excellence to our communities, our colleagues, our customers, and even to our competitors."

Before World War II, few American office buildings were considered to be examples of innovative architecture. Some notable exceptions to the dull industrial architecture of the day would be the Chrysler Building in New York City, some of the Louis Sullivan buildings in Chicago, and buildings here and there which entrepreneurs had built which were good but not sensational.

So when my father commissioned Frank Lloyd Wright to design an office building for Johnson Wax in 1936, it was a unique event. That decision marked my father as a kind of visionary, because his choice was a financial as well as an architectural gamble. Back in those days, our company was relatively small, with only $15 to $20 million in sales. To put the decision he made into perspective, the cost of the building proved to be equal to one and one-half years' total profits of the company! And what he got is one of the greatest buildings of the modern age.

My father's choice of Frank Lloyd Wright as the architect for the Administration Building was indeed a courageous move. An aura of controversy surrounded Wright at the time. He was well known for his famous prairie homes, which he began designing in the early 1900s, and for the earthquake-proof Imperial Hotel in Tokyo, but he had done little significant work in over a decade.

At the time Wright got the commission to build our Administration Building, he was just about broke. He had not had much work because of the Depression, and his public image had suffered from media reports about his personal life. And, by the time of his selection by my father, he also had developed a degree of arrogance and was not the

Frank Lloyd Wright designed the Johnson Wax Administration Building in 1936; construction was completed in 1939. Changes in the building include carpeting and a brass rail around the mezzanine. Basically, however, the building has not changed since it was built.

most popular figure among his peers in the world of architecture. He had a saying on this point, which I love as one of his most famous quotations: "Very early in my life, I had to choose between honest arrogance and hypocritical humility, and I chose honest arrogance."

When H.F. went up to Spring Green, Wisconsin, to meet Frank Lloyd Wright for the first time, they got along famously, although there were reports of minor insults passed back and forth. While my father was a very practical businessman, he had a bit of artistic flair about him. He had fairly good drawing skills and did some minor painting.

My father had an image for the new administrative center: He wanted a building where the people who worked there could be happy. Wright proved to be the perfect architect for realizing that image. He wanted to eliminate the drabness and dullness of the typical American workplace by creating an uplifting and invigorating work environment.

My father also wanted to build something that would set us apart. He was tired of the company being known as a little old family enterprise in a little town in the Midwest. I think he reasoned that erecting a spectacular office building would be a way of refuting that small town image. Whether that was the reason, or whether he wanted to do something that was distinguished by its excellence alone, I really don't know. I think it may have been a combination of the two.

The building which Frank Lloyd Wright designed for my father broke new ground in the design of industrial workspace and in building construction. The Administration Building was unique and daring not only in how it would look, but also in how it would work. Wright designed an integrated unit, in which every detail shared his design conception, down to the door knobs. The form of the building reflected the structure of the company. Modular furniture and an open office concept were employed—decades before they became common. New materials were used in the construction; some even had to be invented to meet the unique demands of the structure.

Not everyone shared the vision which my father and Wright had for the administration building, though. Among the doubters was the Wisconsin Industrial Commission, which refused approval of the building plans, charging that the design of the columns in the Great Workroom was unsafe. The Commission didn't believe that the columns, which were only nine inches wide at their bases, would be strong enough to support the roof of the enormous building. When a single column withstood a load of sixty tons—ten times its required endurance—at a worksite showdown, the state allowed construction to continue.

Wright and my father, along with hundreds of on-lookers, were witnesses to this dramatic field test. My father loved to build things, to be part of a building, a company, whatever. He loved to watch progress, and so it was with the Administration Building: He watched it go up, brick by brick. That building did set us apart. It garnered

Wingspread, the former home of Mr. & Mrs. H. F. Johnson, now the conference center for The Johnson Foundation, was designed by Frank Lloyd Wright.

wide attention and much publicity—and still does. And just as important, it sparked the interest and the pride of our community; 26,000 local citizens toured the building on the opening day.

Life magazine gave it space, too, and even gave it the nod over our big-city rivals. The 1939 World's Fair had opened in New York the same week our building opened, and the *Life* review said, ". . .the Fair, with all its sprawling mass of freak and futuristic buildings, is an undeniably great show. But future historians may well decide that a truer glimpse of the shape of things to come was given last week by a single structure, built strictly for business, which was opened in a drab section of Racine, Wisconsin."

But my father's commitment to excellence in architecture also had a very personal side. For Frank Lloyd Wright was not designing just a company building during his stint at Racine in the 1930s; he was also commissioned at that time to design a house for my father and his family. "Wingspread," as the house was called, became every bit the architectural landmark that the Administration Building did. Wright himself called it an experiment in design and construction. And my father became well acquainted with Wright's "honest arrogance" during the first few years in the house, as certain innovations proved difficult to live with, and Wright proved resistant to any "tampering" with his design.

Mr. H. F. Johnson, left, had great respect and admiration for Frank Lloyd Wright, and their relationship during the construction of the Johnson Wax Administration Building and the Research Tower is well documented.

The Council House is the company's international conference center, opened in 1979, which serves as an informal gathering place for employees and guests from all over the world to discuss business, social, community, and governmental concerns. It was designed by Robert G. Wirth.

Some of their interchanges have become legendary, but none is as vivid to me as the leaky roof at Wingspread. At a formal dinner party, which as a thirteen-year-old I was privileged to attend, a sudden thunderstorm sent a stream of water down on my father's head as he presided over the table. In righteous anger, he summoned a telephone and put through a call to Wright out in Phoenix, Arizona. Only minutes later he was telling Wright how Wingspread was beautiful, but it had a leaky roof and water was leaking right on top of his head! Wright's reply was loud enough for us all to hear: "Well, Hib, why don't you move your chair?"

Europlant, at Mijdrecht, the Netherlands, features a boomerang that projects over a reflecting pond. The architects were H. A. Maaskant and Herman Senf.

THE JOHNSON FOUNDATION
WINGSPREAD.

Great Moments
IN
Architecture:
Frank Lloyd Wright
finally solves
the leak problem
at Wingspread.

Despite such difficulties, for my father, sister, and me it was a happy place to live. Today Wingspread is the conference center for The Johnson Foundation, and the home that my father loved is providing an inspirational setting for conferences. Frank Lloyd Wright said that Wingspread turned out to be a "veritable thing of the Spirit." The spirit has stayed within the house, first as a private and now as a public place.

Wingspread was not the end of the creative partnership between my father and Frank Lloyd Wright. In the early 1940s, my father decided that the company was going to need additional research space after the end of the war. Company officers and scientists pressed hard for a functional facility, designed by an architect well-versed in the ins and outs of building a laboratory. My father finally bowed to their judgment, but Frank Lloyd Wright did not take lightly the company's decision to use a "conventional" architect for such an important commission. He sent my father three typically brash letters, outlining a visionary tower. Over the objections of his business advisors, my father commissioned Wright to build his tower, and the Johnson Research Tower was opened in 1950. It is a wonderful building, a single shaft with cantilevered square and round floors alternating with each other. We have way outgrown it and most all of our research and development is carried out in other buildings. But it is still a symbol of our dedication to excellence and creativity.

The Administration Building-Tower complex continues to catch the public's imagination. Even though the Frank Lloyd Wright buildings are in some ways less functional than they were in 1939, compared with what might be done today with new materials and new concepts of office layout, our buildings still stand as exciting works of art in their time and in our time. And it is sad that the Research Tower couldn't continue to be used for its original purpose because of limited space. On the other hand, it still stands, as Mr. Wright said it would in his impetuous letters to my father, as ". . . a torch lifting to the sky to inspire your people around the world."

The tradition of architectural excellence which my father started in 1936 has proven just as durable as the landmarks he built in Racine. Our buildings have come to symbolize both our commitment to high business standards and our commitment to the communities and countries in which we operate. We have found that this is true even in our recent diversifications and acquisitions. We don't have to start with expensive facilities when we establish a company, but it is interesting to note that our companies never seem to get rolling until we get a good place for them to live—an architecturally good building to operate in! Really great companies today don't build "mean" little buildings, or "mean" big buildings, for that matter. They construct buildings that their people are proud of.

Seeking excellence in architecture has extended all around the world. Just as back in 1936 we got the best American architect to build our new facilities in Racine, in our international operations we made decisions to grant commissions for new buildings to the best architects of our host countries. The results have been terrific, in a business and a public relations sense. I used to get kidded about "Sam's Boomerang"—the Johnson Europlant in the Netherlands designed by the Dutch firm of Maaskant, Van Dommelen, Kroos and Senf—but that office building has focused a good deal of favorable interest on our operations in that country.

Our office and warehouse complex in France, an excellent design by the fine French architect Marc Nebinger, has gotten a similar favorable response. Nebinger created the Croix-de-Lorraine de Colombey-les-deux—Eglises, a monument to Charles DeGaulle. In building our new facility, we worked closely with the French government and their planners in their drive to encourage modern industrialization without disfiguring or destroying Paris or other historic cities. French Johnson headquarters are in Cergy-Pontoise, one of five "New Cities" on the outskirts of Paris.

Our corporate and personal commitment to excellence and innovation hasn't led us to a simple-minded pattern of "modern" architecture. I am particularly proud of the restorations and reconversions we have undertaken at various places around the world. An excellent example in Racine is the Louis Laboratory, where we converted an empty hospital into a modern research facility. This adaptive reuse got us much-needed, high-quality research and office space in a shorter time and at a lower cost than building a new facility. In England we took a rather contemporary (by English standards) manor house, Harewood House, and turned it into our Eurocentre headquarters. Nearby, we rehabilitated historic Milton Park, a building with antecedents in the twelfth century, into a modern laboratory, while at the same time preserving the architectural quality of the building.

As the company has diversified, buildings and real estate have become a part of our business, rather than just a setting for our business. The Johnson Wax Development Corporation, a subsidiary formed in 1971, has developed residential and commercial properties across the country. For me, the most significant of these is perhaps the Council House, an international conference center north of Racine. Its design evokes the historic Wisconsin architecture of which Wingspread, the last of Wright's prairie houses, is perhaps the greatest example.

If I were to single out the most important business-related benefits of the fine architecture that Johnson Wax has been associated with, both here and overseas, it is the impact such architecture has on the people in the company and the advantage it provides in attracting better people to join the company. I think my father, too, perceived early on that architecture can be important in a collective, corporate sense as well as in an individual sense. In the collective sense, we want our buildings to convey our commitment of excellence to our communities, our colleagues, our customers, and even to our competitors. In the individual sense, the physical environment in which people work is an important part of the way they work, an important part of their productivity as individuals, and a contributing factor to their creativity. We will seek to uphold our tradition of excellence whenever we build.

Our commitment to excellence in architecture is not limited strictly to business, though, as Wingspread shows. And in our broad support of architecture—whether in endowing buildings or in supporting museum exhibits which can communicate the potential of fine architecture to broad audiences—we owe much to the example of my father. The Herbert F. Johnson Museum of Art at Cornell University, dedicated in 1973, is a testament to my father's enduring vision of architecture and the arts.

From a commanding setting on a knoll on the Ithaca campus, the I. M. Pei-designed building stands as a giant lens and provides a home for much of Cornell's art collection. In making the gift which made the spectacular building possible, my father spoke of his hopes for the new building, stressing the importance he placed on the integration of the arts with all phases of life. The Cornell museum, and the many other significant buildings with which he was associated, show the strength of his personal commitment:

> It is my hope that the new museum will serve the students of Cornell, at present and in the future, as a wider window on the world of fine arts, enabling them to add a broader dimension to their lives no matter what their fields of study might be. A full appreciation and study of the arts can provide a deep enrichment of one's own life, and especially in today's world it can help us strengthen our respect for the dignity and individual creativity of every person.

ART—ENHANCING THE QUALITY OF LIFE

*"Over the past few decades, we have seen a new partner
emerge in support of the arts—the corporation."*

The idea that art can improve human existence and that the arts should be open and accessible to all is at least as old as the Roman republic. This vision of the arts has been the mission of countless anonymous, renowned, and notorious individuals and assemblages. For over two thousand years the church and the state and, later, the private collector have supported the arts, from the forgotten craftsmen of the medieval cathedrals, to the magnificent patronage of the Medicis, to the art acquisitions of the nineteenth century American railroad millionaires.

Over the past few decades, we have seen a new partner emerge in the support of the arts—the corporation. This movement is one which Johnson Wax pioneered and has continued to lead.

Our support of the arts—as with so many other of our innovations— owes much to the leadership of my father. Its direct roots lie in my father's decision to employ Frank Lloyd Wright to design the new Johnson Wax administration building and then his home, Wingspread. These decisions had as much to do with aesthetics as with business, and they resulted in a remarkable creative partnership between Wright and my father.

As my father's and Wright's working partnership continued, my father's enthusiasm for the arts grew. The benefits of this support of the creative arts quickly moved from a personal commitment on one man's part to a corporate commitment on the part of Johnson Wax. Over the years we have supported such varied disciplines as painting, sculpture, craftsmanship, and filmmaking. Art has become an important and vital part of our corporate environment.

We have found that good art in the workplace is a creative stimulus to the people who spend time there. And it is, like Wright's buildings, a symbol of the company's pursuit of excellence. By sponsoring artistic people, we demonstrate an appreciation for high standards—and hope that such goals pervade the atmosphere around us.

Though the idea is common now, prior to the 1960s few

corporations had an interest in the arts. Today, of course, many corporations purchase art, sponsor touring exhibits, and support all manners of artistic pursuits. There is even a group called "The Business Committee for the Arts," an organization of companies that works to foster support for such endeavors. But two decades ago there was little interaction between corporate America and the creative community.

In 1962 the company assembled ART:USA, the Johnson Collection of Contemporary American Painting. It included 102 paintings by 102 living American artists. We purchased the paintings and sent the exhibit on a two-year tour of eighteen cities around the world. Following that, the company sponsored another two-and-a-half year tour, this time through twenty-five American cities. ART:USA received exceptional acclaim and broke museum attendance records wherever it was exhibited.

Conceived as an act of faith in American art, ART:USA also was something of an experiment. Because of the international tour, we had wondered what kind of impact it might have on our relations with people in other countries. And since it was one of the first large corporate exhibits of its type, I believe that ART:USA served as a keystone in legitimizing business support of the arts.

All things considered, ART:USA was not even that costly. We carefully selected each painting. By the time the tour was finished, the collection was worth much more than we had originally paid, and we donated it to the Smithsonian as a charitable contribution. But of greater importance to us was that ART:USA reached people around the world, was something the company and its people could be proud of, and enhanced Johnson's reputation for doing the unusual in the name of excellence.

The company's next large artistic venture was commissioned for the New York World's Fair in 1964. My father said that though the company was involved in the 1939 Fair in only a small way, he had had a lot of fun there and wanted to do it again. And that is how we came to build the Johnson Wax Golden Rondelle.

We had decided that a film would be shown in the Golden Rondelle, and my father wanted the best documentary filmmaker around, just as he had wanted the best architect and landed Frank Lloyd Wright. He found that the filmmaker he sought was Francis Thompson.

Thompson came to see my father and they had a private conference. My father told Mr. Thompson to make the film.

The rest of us had little idea of what had transpired between them. And we were already upset with the basic idea of spending $5 million on the Fair. All we knew about the film was that it would be upbeat and would concern life in the United States and abroad. Finally, I felt I had to ask my father for a few more details.

"Well," he said, "I'm sick and tired of all this beatnik stuff [recall this was 1962], and everyone being down on the United States and the world. Really, there are many more nice things going on in the world and many more opportunities for fun and good living than there ever were before. I want a movie that has a very positive view on life." He concluded his short speech by saying that Francis Thompson had understood his vision.

"But didn't you work out any more details than that?" I asked. "Didn't you get a script?"

"Don't worry about the details or a script. This is a good man, Sam. I can tell. He will give us a good film. Now don't worry about it."

Nearly two years passed and the Golden Rondelle was nearing completion. Then, about three weeks before the Fair was to open, we were invited to Francis Thompson's little studio on New York's Third Avenue. There he had rigged up three small screens, so we could see what he had done.

A book illustrated with stills from the motion picture "To Be Alive!" was published by Johnson Wax in 1966, after the film's outstanding success at the New York World's Fair 1964-65.

ART:USA toured for two years in eighteen cities around the world, and then for another two-and-a-half years in twenty-five American cities.

Neither the narration nor the music was complete. "I just want to give you a flavor of it," said Thompson. What we saw was a series of scenes appearing on the three screens: people dancing, people rowing boats—you could tell right off that the camera work was excellent, but you really couldn't get much flavor of the film's tone. Sensing our mood, my father turned around and said, "Don't worry about it. Francis knows what he is doing."

Virtually all of us were discouraged; some were discouraged even more than we were on the day the film was commissioned. "Are we going to have a press party for the grand opening?" asked my father. No one answered. "Get public relations to organize the whole thing, and I want all of the big-time press people in New York to come out and see it."

"But what if it's a stinker?" I asked. "Then where are you?"

"Don't worry about it! Francis is an artist."

And indeed he was. When the media gathered in the Rondelle for the initial presentation of "To Be Alive," it was a first viewing for all of us. The film practically blew everyone out of the seats. It was perhaps the finest piece of cinematography of its type ever produced.

"To Be Alive" was a major hit at the World's Fair. It, and the Golden Rondelle, gave the company tremendous publicity and helped elevate the firm's reputation. Even today people mention it to me. In 1966, "To Be Alive" won an Oscar from the Academy of Motion Picture Arts and Sciences as the best documentary short subject. It was featured again in the United Nations Pavilion at Expo-67 in Montreal. And it is still shown in our Racine reconstruction of the Golden Rondelle.

ART:USA and "To Be Alive" were tremendous successes which began to broaden our horizons and the range of our involvement with

Non-functional items were an outstanding feature of OBJECTS:USA, the Johnson Collection of Contemporary Crafts, which toured the United States and overseas for several years after it was assembled in 1968. Mrs. S. C. Johnson (Gene, far right) hosted the opening reception in Washington.

In 1962, the company took a leadership position by assembling ART:USA, the Johnson Collection of Contemporary American Painting. Among those attending the Washington, D.C. premiere were then Vice President and Mrs. Lyndon B. Johnson.

art. So, in 1968 we formed a new collection, only this time the focus was on American crafts. Called OBJECTS:USA, the Johnson Collection of Contemporary Crafts included 308 pieces by 258 Americans.

It was, to be sure, an ecletic group of items, covering a wide range of media, including wood, ceramics, jewelry, fabric, glass, and metal.

Each object was the product of an individual's craftsmanship. OBJECTS:USA's purposes were to focus attention on singular achievements and to stimulate interest in this special field of individual creativity.

Within the realm of arts, contemporary crafts were considered second-class citizens. Many items never had been truly recognized as works of art, except perhaps in the antique world. OBJECTS:USA attempted to raise the status of the craftsperson. We sent the exhibit on a tour of major museums and college campuses in twenty-three cities in the United States. We provided support so that a book could be published on the works. A television documentary called "With These Hands" featured eight of the craftsmen and appeared on ABC in 1970 as an hour-long special.

OBJECTS:USA toured through the U.S. and Europe until 1972, and all of the collection was ultimately contributed to various museums and schools. Many craftsmen told me that the exhibit helped lift crafts out of its second-class image. Today, many crafts are prized by serious collectors and museums. The project furthered crafts as an art form, advanced our company's reputation as a patron of the arts, and increased vital contacts between the businessman and artist, who need each other much more than either realizes.

Other projects followed. In 1976 the company sponsored the first exhibit in the Cooper-Hewitt Museum in New York. With the theme "Man Transforms," the basic idea was to help people see and understand design. The museum has exhibits that show why things look the way they do and how they affect our lives through design. "Man Transforms" presented exhibits that featured R. Buckminster Fuller, O.M. Ungers, George Nelson, and Nader Ardalan, among others. Assembled by Hans Hollein, the exhibit ran for four months and was seen by a half-million people.

To celebrate the nation's Bicentennial we turned again to Francis Thompson, who produced a film called "American Years." We also asked him to make a film, "Living Planet," which we donated as a public service to the National Air and Space Museum in Washington, D.C., and we cosponsored with NASM another Thompson film, "On the Wing." Both are fine films that are being shown at the museum. They also are shown daily at the Golden Rondelle in Racine.

The company's commitment to art also led us to sponsor displays in the Council House, our International Conference Center and Guest House. My sister, Karen, acquired the collection, traveling worldwide to the lands where we had subsidiaries. Our subsidiary companies contributed the art to the Council House.

We could have had the subsidiaries simply send in the artwork, but we wanted a diversity and synthesis that could be achieved only by having a single person do the selecting. Moreover, we had more trust in Karen's artistic taste than in that of the subsidiary managers.

A budget was worked out for each country and company, based on their earnings. Karen had the impression that she was to meet or exceed the budget amount in each country, and did so. "You'll be happy to know I wasn't below budget in any country!" she proudly announced upon her return. "As a matter of fact, I had to buy two or three things in order to get over budget in some places."

This was, perhaps, all for the best. What she found has turned what might have been a conventional guest house and conference center into an exciting place to be. She also was a great emissary for the family, and in fact continued on the project, helping to produce and

Among artists represented in OBJECTS:USA was J.B. Blunk, of California.

Karen Johnson Boyd, daughter of H. F. Johnson, was commissioned to purchase works of art from the forty-five nations where Johnson Wax operates, for exhibition in the new Council House. With her is Dante Santos, Independent Director of Philippines Johnson.

publish a book about the art she had collected.

We have been involved in these special projects, and also are resolved to support the arts on a regular basis. The Johnson's Wax Fund, Inc., gives money to The Racine Art Association, the Smithsonian Institution, The American Crafts Council, the United Performing Arts Fund, Inc., the Racine Symphony Orchestra, and many other groups. We sponsored a special exhibit at the National Gallery of Art on the works of John F. Peto and underwrote a film on the American artist.

I believe that a commitment to the arts should continue in the future, as it does now in our corporate life, as an integral element in our environment. Art is, for what it gives back, an inexpensive investment. And one can never go wrong by paying for quality.

We try to pick the finest examples of an art, a craft, or building design. As Bill Connolly, who was once the company's Vice President of Public Relations, said, "If you can't afford the best, you cannot afford what is not good. The cheap thing may be the most expensive. Good taste, good design, and good judgment should characterize your buildings, your advertising, your packages. As Isaac Disraeli once observed, 'It is wretched taste to be satisfied with mediocrity when excellence lies before us.' "

That is what our involvement in art is—doing things right, creating an environment in which people can do their best and be the most creative. For us it began with Frank Lloyd Wright. I am convinced that without the influence of art and how it symbolizes excellence, we would not be the company we are today.

THOUGHTS ABOUT MONEY AND OTHER THINGS

"It isn't how much money you make during your lifetime that is important, but rather what you do with that money."

My father believed in the basic philosophy that the family business was the most important thing to carry on, not so much for its monetary values that it will create for that family, but for the values of a fine enterprise in and of itself and for the joys of running your own business. The learning process in running your own business is learning how to manage your own money, in order to be assured that in the long term your inheritance of the business is always going to be there.

As a young man, my father saw to it that I learned two important lessons. In the first instance, he worked it out so I learned to handle money responsibly even in my teens. It was expected of me. It has been arranged in my family originally by my father and now by myself that my children never have to ask me for money personally. They can go to their trusts for money, in some cases discuss the withdrawals with trustees. There have no doubt been some things they would liked to have done but didn't do because they didn't have the money to do it. They would never think of coming to ask me for money, except maybe for a joint venture that they wanted me to participate in. They knew that they had their birthrights set up by their grandfather, that the funds were there and would become more important over the years.

Some parents use money as a disciplinary reward or hold-back. As a parent, I found it best to separate discipline from money by removing money from our parent-child equation. Gene and I spent our time around the table talking with our children about what they were going to do with their lives and how they could become productive citizens.

A second important lesson which my father passed along to me was the idea of learning how to be a producer, not just a consumer of things. His concept was that you should earn some money of your own, produce some goods of your own, or paint some paintings of your own. He arranged that I should work at the company during the summertime, which I did, with the exception of the year that I worked for the Horlick Malted Milk Company. My father was a strong adherent to the idea that you should do something that puts more into society than you take out.

As wealth is accumulated it becomes an element of growing concern. It can make a family stronger or destroy a family. It isn't how much money you make during your lifetime that is important, but rather what you do with that money, such as doing something significant for society as well as taking care of the long-term needs of your family.

My father did a great many good things with his money. In fact, he left a very small estate with no Johnson stock in it. He developed a great foundation and conference center at Wingspread and supported many things of a charitable nature in Racine and around the world.

There is an old saying that says "money corrupts." But, in reality, it depends on what you do with it. It can corrupt a young person if it isn't handled right with that young person. It can corrupt the person who is only interested in piling up millions of dollars on top of other millions. But if your objective is to have young people, including your own children, be highly creative, productive members of society, money can help in terms of a good education, staking them to a business venture, or helping them pursue their own creative activities.

If accumulated personal wealth is used as my father used it—in support of Cornell, The Prairie School and at Wingspread, and many other charities—it can be a very positive creative force rather than a corrupting one.

Many a person who has founded a business faces a problem when his heir comes into the company business. I find that the problem is easier to face in a big company than it would be in a small one. The big company is based on more than one successful idea. You have a variety of courses to follow. Each generation has something new to bring to the company, something new to the party. At first, I didn't realize that was the reason I was happy in my career in this business; I had brought something new to it and kept that spirit throughout. I brought new products and diversification to our company. It has been a rewarding experience.

I also established other enterprises outside the mainstream of the S. C. Johnson Wax Company, as part of the family diversification.

One of these enterprises is banking. My father had a piece of land near Wingspread, at a main intersection that he thought would make a good commercial location. The thing I thought it would be best for was a bank. I tried to convince some local bankers and a bank in Milwaukee to put a branch there, but they didn't think it was a very good location. I happened to think it was a great location, so in 1970

The Wind Point office of the Heritage Bank & Trust.

we established a bank on that corner, in a trailer, with a staff of three. It has become the largest bank in Racine, and, over the years, has become the largest bank group outside of Milwaukee in southeastern Wisconsin.

In 1976, we acquired a bank in Geneva, Switzerland. That bank also has flourished, and our whole banking group in time will become a cornerstone of our family's interests, and may provide a career interest for a member of the next generation.

Similarly, Johnson Worldwide Associates is an enterprise which, as I noted earlier, has been taken public. As a public enterprise, JWA gives the family greater liquidity and protects the S. C. Johnson Wax shares that the family holds from being sold to the public to pay inheritance taxes.

As I said, each generation brings something different to the enterprise. In reviewing what my children have brought, this is what I see: Our oldest son, Curt, brought a venture capital business to the company, which so far has been a beneficial diversification to the total operation, because it gives us insights into many new, growing, small businesses and technologies. Our daughter Helen has brought advertising expertise after working for an important advertising agency in Chicago for six years prior to coming to the company in marketing. Our son Fisk, who is a PhD scientist and an MBA businessman, has brought the outlook of a businessman/scientist, just as his grandfather did. And, our youngest daughter, Win, working in Public Affairs on special assignments, brought her skills of dealing with the public, and she is further developing her talents in this area.

They all seem happy working with the family group now. It may be that some one or more of them will one day pursue their own careers elsewhere. I am, however, confident that among this next generation are members who will be involved in continuing these great family enterprises. And with four young grandchildren growing up, I am fairly confident that we can remain a family enterprise through yet another generation.

An important question arises: With all this diversification, and with four members of the fifth generation in my family and four members in my sister's—each having a financial interest in the family enterprises—how does everyone stay glued together yet moving forward in a constructive and creative way?

One answer has been a "Family Office." Nine years ago, I decided that we needed to have a financial focal point for my sister and me and for the members of our family. So we established a family office to provide confidential help to the family. This help is in the form of professional tax, legal, and estate planning advice, business advice on other enterprises members might be interested in, and general

The bank in Geneva, Switzerland.

administrative support of the various family activities.

The family office concept has worked very well. Because the individuals on the staff have a confidential relationship with each member of the family, members feel comfortable about using it. We have a rule that neither my sister nor I should be informed what others in the family are doing, unless they choose to inform us, or unless they ask for our help or advice. This allows each family member privacy, but still insures that everyone is well served and that things they want to do are supported and are consistent with the continuation of the family enterprises.

In my father's day, when there were only my sister and myself, and I was the only one active in the business, things were much simpler, and a family office was not necessary. But with the business diversifications and the varied interests of family members, I wonder now how we ever got by successfully without it.

The essential element of the family office is the confidential and professional way that it serves the family. Everyone still is the master of his or her own affairs; it is seldom that I'm called upon to enter into a matter that isn't strictly my own, or of general family interest.

Finally, I think the family comes first. If you take care of your family responsibilities in the right way, there is a better chance the children will become productive members of society, not socialites or playboys. There is a lot you can do by example and close contacts with your children over the years.

A TRIBUTE TO HFJ

*"My father did as much as any of the Johnsons in shaping
the way the company is today."*

As should be obvious by now, there are dozens of central ideas that influence the goals and guide the corporate behavior of S. C. Johnson & Son. Many of these ideas are wise and farsighted. Most also contain a strong dose of common sense. These ideas help bind the company together, and to an extent, they govern the way it treats people. These precepts are the philosophical rudder of the enterprise, and many were first articulated within the company by my father, H. F. Johnson, Jr.

My father died late in 1978, nearly fourteen years after a stroke had impaired his speech and limited some of the function in his right arm and leg. He loved to talk and he loved the outdoors, so these afflictions frustrated him greatly. Yet he continued to express his vision for the company. His strength, determination, and ideas are still with us today.

If you have read this collection of essays you already will know much about HFJ, Jr., and his approach to business, people, and life. I came to understand a large number of my basic beliefs from watching and listening to him. My father, of course, learned much from his father, who in turn had learned from his father, the founder of the parquet floor business. Therefore, in a very special sense each reader will find—albeit subliminally—a certain continuity across the generations within these pages. This is a Johnson tradition, if you will, that goes back to the 1800s.

My father did as much as any of the Johnsons in shaping the way the company is today. I can point to six major elements of his character—among many others, of course—which in particular helped to guide, mold, and inspire the enterprise. I choose these anecdotes and descriptions because I believe they are the traits that most affected the business and a great number of people in the most significant of ways:

• *My father was a scientist*, and indisputably proud of it. In fact, he was S. C. Johnson & Son's first trained chemist, a graduate of Cornell University. He took his new postgraduate job with admirable dedication, going so far as to convert the toilet in the old office building into a laboratory. He created work space where he could find it.

It was because of his scientific background, I think, that he came up with the notion of Product Plus, a conviction that nifty packaging, slick advertising, and all the other tools of marketing were not enough for a new product. He believed that for a new product to really work, it must have some technological edge, some characteristic that made it superior to whatever else existed.

He was the father of technology at Johnson Wax. As our business increasingly becomes driven by rapidly changing technologies, we are fortunate that he placed us on a scientific path long ago.

• *He was an internationalist*, following in the footsteps of his father, to be sure, but also traveling to places where few other American businessmen had trod. HFJ took trips to far places in the days when transportation was much less reliable than it is today.

In 1935, for example, he took his twin-motor Sikorsky amphibian—an aircraft that took off at ninety miles-per-hour, flew at ninety, and landed at ninety—all the way to Brazil. He and four of his associates

H. F. Johnson Jr.

simply left for three months. In some family businesses this would have led straight to disaster, but my father had created an organization he could trust. Therefore, he had the ability to travel, enjoy himself, and still take care of the business details of an overseas journey.

He also had a knack for finding good people outside the United States, and he carried a fundamental faith that Johnson Wax would one day be exceptionally strong in the international arena. I think he believed that by making corporate global connections we could place diverse people in touch with each other, and that in some way this would contribute to world peace.

• *He was a creative leader*, a man who insisted on the best and devised ingenious means to draw superior performance from his people. I mentioned his use of Booz, Allen and Hamilton and how he believed in the benefits of retaining wise consultants and counsel. Well, he once set Booz, Allen and Hamilton after me.

One day he told me the consultants would be conducting a new survey, and that it would be about me. "I think you're a pretty good young man," he explained, "and some of my associates agree. But I really don't know if we have the right plan for you to be able eventually

While on a tour of McDonnell Aircraft, H. F. Johnson had an opportunity to sit at the controls of a Mercury space craft. The association between James McDonnell, Jr. and H.F. went back to the early days when McDonnell Aircraft was just beginning and H.F. financially assisted the aircraft designer in his first venture.

to take over leadership of the company. I want Booz to look at you—to look at the kind of career track you should be taking—so we'll have a solid plan, based on the best opinions available, for you to follow."

He wasn't kidding. The consultants conducted a survey and prepared a report that came in one of those gold-embossed Booz, Allen and Hamilton black books. It had my name right under a title that said "Career Plans." And because it flatly laid out my strengths

A bronze bust of H. F. Johnson, created by Jimilu Mason. The figure is now prominently located in the lobby of the Administration Building, mounted on a walnut pedestal which resembles one of the columns in the Great Workroom.

Called into government service, H. F. Johnson served during 1954-55 in Washington, D.C. as Director of the Office of Industrial Resources of the Foreign Operations Administration, which was headed up during the Eisenhower Administration by Harold E. Stassen, left.

and weaknesses, it turned out to be a valuable document. My father used creative leadership to state points that I might otherwise have never listened to.

HFJ had an amazing memory and was a perfectionist when it came to details. Therefore, he was nearly impossible to bluff. He was an expert in asking what the Management Committee deemed the "wrong" question—a question that no one on the Committee could answer, but the solution of which usually was an important part of the success of whatever we were discussing.

It got so that everyone on the Management Committee feared getting trapped by another HFJ question. We all began bringing bigger and bigger piles of reference documents, to the point where the Committee would convene at a table full of two-foot high stacks of paper. "This place is beginning to look like a bloody library," my father observed one morning. "Would you gentlemen please do your homework outside of the meeting room so we can get down to business!"

Although he could tear holes in a weak argument, HFJ was hardly a complete autocrat. His leadership skills involved getting a consensus on most decisions. Only once in awhile would he operate exclusively

In 1957, H. F. Johnson was honored by the Brazilian government with the National Order of the Southern Cross, the highest award that the country gives to a non-Brazilian. Doing the honors in a ceremony in Washington, D.C. was Brazilian Ambassador Ernani Do Amaral Peixoto.

H. F. Johnson, right, followed the construction of the Administration Building firsthand. Seated on a pile of lumber are, from left, Wes Peters, Taliesen architect, Frank Lloyd Wright, and Johnson.

on his own hunches—and make a singular decision. But those usually were whoppers, like the New York World's Fair of 1964-65 and the exhibit and film that cost Johnson Wax more than $5 million and earned the company uncountable sums in good publicity and goodwill.

• *He was a humanist*, who truly believed it when he said, "People are our most valuable resource." He also said, "Even though this business has grown to many times its original size, we have never permitted it to outweigh or submerge the individual."

He believed in the good of individual creativity and in the dignity of man and woman. He also thought of the community in much the same way. He frequently said, "Every community where we operate should become a better place because we are there," if only to ensure we all understood.

This is a primary reason he insisted that Johnson Wax give five percent of its before-tax earnings to charities and community organizations. While altruistic, it also helped the firm by nurturing its surroundings. He once told me that very few people knew how to make money with one hand and spend it with the other. He believed that in some ways it was harder to give money away wisely than to make it.

H. F. Johnson had a lifelong interest in hunting and fishing. He and his father, Herbert Fisk Johnson (right), landed this catch off Catalina Island in 1909 when he was only ten.

An American business journal once described H. F. Johnson as a "pleasant, rather shy man who loves hunting and fishing." Fly-fishing along rushing streams was among his favorite sports, like this instance in 1962.

My father was a businessman first and foremost. But he cared so much about these humanistic concerns that on occasions I wondered whether the business, to him, simply supported some greater effort, however much subordinate to business it appeared on the surface.

• *He was a family man*, who despite the pressures of the business liked to do things with his family. For example, he took me to England when I was eleven years old. I also remember our times together hunting and fishing. He was one of the quickest bird shots I have ever seen. And in quiet moments he would put down his shotgun and draw sketches of birds and animals he had seen in the field.

HFJ also believed that young people, particularly his own children, should go to work early in life. He would allow me to lie around the house for two to three days into the summer vacation, but then I would be pressed for employment at the Waxworks. I worked in the lab, the shipping department, and other places. For the first three summers the pay was pretty darn low.

Between my junior and senior years of high school I met old A. J. Horlick, a family friend who owned Horlick's Malted Milk Company. With a gleam in his eye he asked me what I was making at the Waxworks and then offered me a much higher wage to come work in his lab. I took the job. Although Horlick, wherever he may be, probably still is chortling over his pirating of HFJ's son, I am not sure my father ever fully forgave me for that summer. And yet, maybe he understood.

• *He was a man with vision*—an all-important, long-range vision. He seldom thought only in terms of months or years, but of entire generations. He wanted to plan the company's future so that it would support the next generation as much as the current. He planned his estate and succession of ownership long before his death. He started training me long before I had left my youth.

In 1953 he wrote me a letter that was to be opened upon his death. I was but a brash first lieutenant in the Air Force, and he would live another twenty-five years. There was no urgency to write that letter. Yet even under those conditions his words were as meaningful as if he had written them knowing he had only a day to live.

"Remember to treat kindly the people who have been so faithful and loyal to us for years," he wrote near the end of the letter. "Some of them may try to challenge you by saying you are not doing as well as your grandfather or father did. This is something you shouldn't give any worry to because what your great-grandfather, grandfather, and I did was to build on a foundation of honesty and integrity in business. And this has made our business as successful as it is today. Just go ahead in the way you think best, honestly and justly building on the foundations which the members of the Johnson family have laid down for you. I'm confident in your future."

HFJ, Jr. did help give me confidence in the future. He certainly gave me a rock-solid foundation on which to work. But of all the things he left me, perhaps the most important was the idea that one should always plan in terms of twenty years hence, that S. C. Johnson & Son must be nurtured today for the generations of tomorrow.

A BIOGRAPHICAL SKETCH OF SAMUEL C. JOHNSON AND IMOGENE POWERS JOHNSON

Samuel C. Johnson was born March 2, 1928 in Racine, Wisconsin. He is a 1950 graduate of Cornell University, receiving his B.A. in economics. He earned his M.B.A. from Harvard Business School in 1952. He also holds honorary doctorate degrees from Carthage College, Kenosha, Wisconsin; Northland College, Ashland, Wisconsin; Ripon College, Ripon, Wisconsin; Carroll College, Waukesha, Wisconsin; University of Surrey, England; and Marquette University, Milwaukee, Wisconsin. He served as a U.S. Air Force intelligence officer from 1952 until 1954.

He joined S. C. Johnson & Son, Inc. (Johnson Wax) in 1954 as Assistant to the President. In 1955 he organized the company's first New Products Department and served as its Director until 1958, leading the company into a program of broad and successful diversification which continues to this day.

In 1958 he became Vice President of the newly organized Service Products Division, and in 1960 was named Vice President and European Regional Director, with headquarters in London. He became International Vice President in 1962, and was elected Executive Vice President in 1963.

In 1966, at the age of thirty-eight, he was elected President, adding the title of Chairman the following year. In 1972 he was elected Chairman and Chief Executive Officer, and served in that position until March 1979, when he relinquished the title of Chief Executive Officer and began an eighteen-month leave of absence to attend to family and estate matters following the death of his father, Herbert F. Johnson, Jr., in December 1978. He resumed his position as Chief Executive Officer in October 1980.

Mr. Johnson is the fourth generation of his family to serve as Chairman of Johnson Wax and he is the great-grandson of his namesake, who founded the company in 1886.

His many philanthropic, educational, and cultural activities include serving as Chairman of the Board of The Johnson Foundation, Inc. and Chairman of The Johnson's Wax Fund, Inc. He is Founding Chairman Emeritus of The Prairie School, Racine.

He also serves as a Trustee Emeritus and Presidential Counselor of Cornell University; Chairman of the Advisory Council, Samuel Curtis Johnson Graduate School of Management at Cornell, which he endowed in honor of his great-grandfather; Chairman of the Board of Trustees, The Mayo Foundation, Rochester, Minnesota; member of the Council of Former Governors, the American Red Cross, and the EAA Aviation Foundation President's Council; and he is a member of The Nature Conservancy International Advisory Committee and a life member of the Nature Conservancy. He is also a member of the Executive Committee & Board of Regents of the Smithsonian Institution, Washington, D.C.

Mr. Johnson serves as a Director of Mobil Corporation; Director of Deere and Company; Director of H. J. Heinz Company; Director and

Gene (Mrs. S. C.) Johnson is one of the founders and is current chairperson of The Prairie School.

Chairman, Johnson Worldwide Associated, Inc.; and Director and Chairman, Heritage Racine Bancorp, Ltd., Racine. He is also a member of The Business Council.

He is a serious nature photographer, avid fisherman, jet and seaplane pilot, and scuba diver.

Sam Johnson met Imogene Powers at Cornell University in 1948. She was a mathematics major, with an important interest in astronomy, which she has continued to pursue. They were married in 1954 after he left the U.S. Air Force and after she had pursued a successful career as an engineering mathematician at Ryan Aeronautical, San Diego, California. She was an early computer programmer, working on the first vertical take-off aircraft, in an era when computers were barely known in the business world.

Gene Johnson subsequently has devoted her time to various not-for-profit activities, including the Racine Area United Way, the YWCA and the YWCA's River Bend Nature Center, Chairperson of The Prairie School, and member of the board of the Laboratory of Ornithology at Cornell. She holds an honorary doctorate from Carroll College, of Waukesha, Wisconsin. She is a serious gardener, and likes tennis and paddle tennis, fishing, canoeing, trekking, and bird-watching.

Mr. & Mrs. Johnson have two sons and two daughters and reside in Racine. —*Serge E. Logan*

GENEALOGY OF THE JOHNSON FAMILY

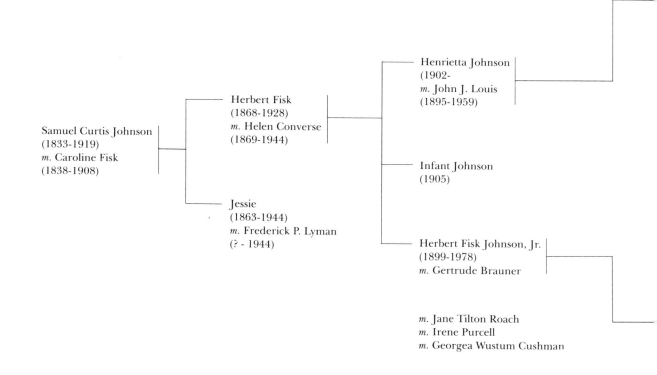

Samuel Curtis Johnson
(1833-1919)
m. Caroline Fisk
(1838-1908)

Herbert Fisk
(1868-1928)
m. Helen Converse
(1869-1944)

Jessie
(1863-1944)
m. Frederick P. Lyman
(? - 1944)

Henrietta Johnson
(1902-
m. John J. Louis
(1895-1959)

Infant Johnson
(1905)

Herbert Fisk Johnson, Jr.
(1899-1978)
m. Gertrude Brauner

m. Jane Tilton Roach
m. Irene Purcell
m. Georgea Wustum Cushman

GENEALOGY OF THE JOHNSON FAMILY

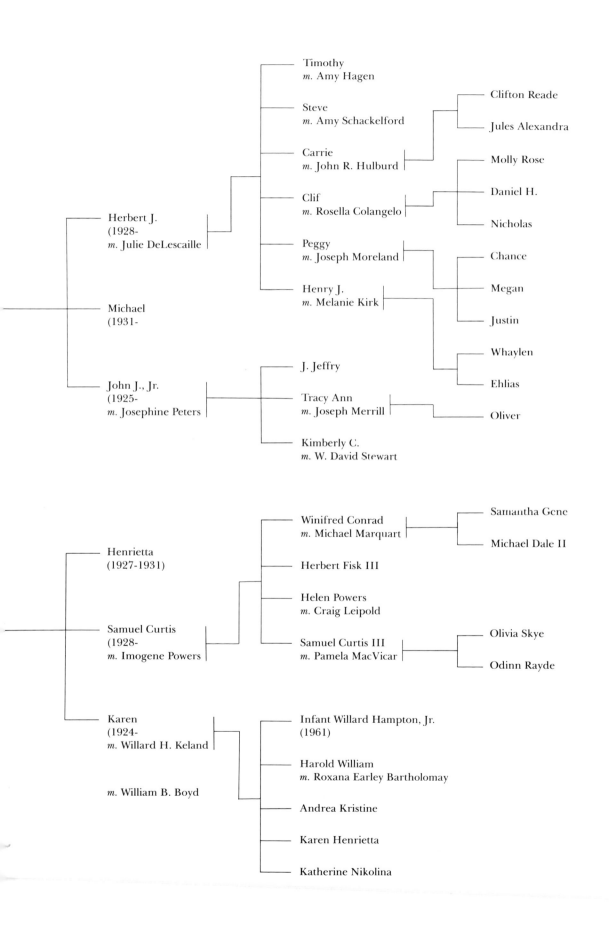

Herbert J.
(1928-
m. Julie DeLescaille

Timothy
m. Amy Hagen

Steve
m. Amy Schackelford

Carrie
m. John R. Hulburd

Clifton Reade

Jules Alexandra

Clif
m. Rosella Colangelo

Molly Rose

Daniel H.

Nicholas

Peggy
m. Joseph Moreland

Chance

Megan

Henry J.
m. Melanie Kirk

Justin

Michael
(1931-

Whaylen

Ehlias

John J., Jr.
(1925-
m. Josephine Peters

J. Jeffry

Tracy Ann
m. Joseph Merrill

Oliver

Kimberly C.
m. W. David Stewart

Henrietta
(1927-1931)

Winifred Conrad
m. Michael Marquart

Samantha Gene

Michael Dale II

Herbert Fisk III

Helen Powers
m. Craig Leipold

Samuel Curtis
(1928-
m. Imogene Powers

Samuel Curtis III
m. Pamela MacVicar

Olivia Skye

Odinn Rayde

Karen
(1924-
m. Willard H. Keland

Infant Willard Hampton, Jr.
(1961)

Harold William
m. Roxana Earley Bartholomay

m. William B. Boyd

Andrea Kristine

Karen Henrietta

Katherine Nikolina

THIS WE BELIEVE

Introduction

Our company has been guided by certain basic principles since its founding in 1886.

These principles were first summarized in 1927 by H. F. Johnson, Sr., in his Christmas Profit Sharing speech:

"The goodwill of the people is the only enduring thing in any business. It is the sole substance . . . The rest is shadow!"

In 1976, we formally stated these basic principles in **"This We Believe."** Since then, our statement of corporate philosophy has been translated and communicated around the world—not only within the worldwide company, but also to key external audiences. It has served us well by providing all employees with a common statement of the basic principles which guide the company in all the different cultures where we operate. It has also provided people outside the company with an understanding of our fundamental beliefs. It communicates the kind of company we are.

Now, more than ten years after **"This We Believe"** was developed and following the celebration of our 100th anniversary, it is appropriate to restate, clarify and reaffirm our commitment to uphold these principles, because our company, like most others in these highly volatile times, has had to adjust its business strategies worldwide. This restatement and clarification is important to assure that our corporate policies and the actions of our managers and other employees continue to be fully supportive of our beliefs.

"This We Believe" states our beliefs in relation to the five groups of people to whom we are responsible and whose trust we have to earn:

Employees

We believe that the fundamental vitality and strength of our worldwide company lies in our people.

Consumers and Users

We believe in earning the enduring goodwill of consumers and users of our products and services.

General Public

We believe in being a responsible leader within the free market economy.

Neighbors and Hosts

We believe in contributing to the well-being of the countries and communities where we conduct business.

World Community

We believe in improving international understanding.

These beliefs are real and we will strive to live up to them. Our commitment to them is evident in our actions to date.

The sincerity of our beliefs encourages us to act with integrity at all times, to respect the dignity of each person as an individual human being, to assume moral and social responsibilities early as a matter of conscience, to make an extra effort to use our skills and resources where they are most needed, and to strive for excellence in everything we do.

Our way of safeguarding these beliefs is to remain a privately held company. Our way of reinforcing them is to make profits through growth and development, profits which allow us to do more for all the people on whom we depend.

We believe that the fundamental vitality and strength of our worldwide company lies in our people, and we commit ourselves to:

Maintain good relations among all employees around the world based on a sense of participation, mutual respect, and an understanding of common objectives, by:

— Creating a climate whereby all employees freely air their concerns and express opinions with the assurance that these will be fairly considered.
— Attentively responding to employees' suggestions and problems.
— Fostering open, two-way communications between management and employees.
— Providing employees with opportunities to participate in the process of decision-making.
— Encouraging employees at all levels and in all disciplines to work as a team.
— Respecting the dignity and rights of privacy of every employee.

Manage our business in such a way that we can provide security for regular employees and retirees, by:

— Pursuing a long-term policy of planned, orderly growth.
— Retaining regular employees, if at all possible, as conditions change. However, this may not always be possible, particularly where major restructuring or reorganization is required to maintain competitiveness.
— Retraining employees who have acceptable performance records and are in positions no longer needed, provided suitable jobs are available.

Maintain a high level of effectiveness within the organization, by:

— Establishing clear standards of job performance.
— Ensuring that the performance of all employees meets required levels by giving appropriate recognition to those whose performance is good and by terminating those whose performance, despite their managers' efforts to help, continues below company standards.

Provide equal opportunities in employment and advancement, by:

— Hiring and promoting employees without discrimination, using qualifications, performance, and experience as the principal criteria.

Remunerate employees at levels that fully reward their performance and recognize their contribution to the success of their company, by:
— Maintaining base pay and benefit programs both of which are fully competitive with those prevailing within the relevant marketplaces.
— Maintaining, in addition to our fully competitive pay and benefit programs, our long-standing tradition of sharing profits with employees.

Protect the health and safety of all employees, by:
— Providing a clean and safe work environment.
— Providing appropriate safety training and occupational health services.

Develop the skills and abilities of our people, by:
— Providing on-the-job training and professional development programs.
— Helping employees qualify for opportunities in the company through educational and development programs.

Create environments which are conducive to self-expression and personal well-being, by:
— Fostering and supporting leisure-time programs for employees and retirees.
— Developing job-enrichment programs.
— Maintaining the long tradition of high quality and good design in our offices and plants.

Encourage initiative, innovation, and entrepreneurism among all employees, thereby providing opportunities for greater job satisfaction while also helping the worldwide company achieve its objectives.

We believe in earning the enduring goodwill of consumers and users of our products and services, and we commit ourselves to:

Provide useful products and services throughout the world, by:
— Monitoring closely the changing wants and needs of consumers and users.
— Developing and maintaining high standards of quality.
— Developing new products and services which are recognized by consumers and users as being significantly superior overall to major competition.
— Maintaining close and effective business relations with the trade to ensure that our products and services are readily available to consumers and users.
— Continuing our research and development commitment to provide a strong technology base for innovative and superior products and services.

Develop and market products which are environmentally sound and which do not endanger the health and safety of consumers and users, by:
— Meeting all regulatory requirements or exceeding them where worldwide company standards are higher.
— Providing clear and adequate directions for safe use, together with cautionary statements and/or symbols.
— Incorporating protection against misuse where this is appropriate.
— Researching new technologies for products which favor an improved environment.

Maintain and develop comprehensive education and service programs for consumers and users, by:
— Disseminating information to consumers and users which promotes full understanding of the correct use of our products and services.
— Handling all inquiries, complaints, and service needs for consumers and users quickly, thoroughly, and fairly.

We believe in being a responsible leader in the free market economy, and we commit ourselves to:

Ensure the future vitality of the worldwide company, by:
— Earning sufficient profits to provide new investment for planned growth and progress.
— Maintaining a worldwide organization of highly competent, motivated, and dedicated employees.

Conduct our business in a fair and ethical manner, by:
— Not engaging in unfair business practices.
— Treating our suppliers and customers both fairly and reasonably, according to sound commercial practice.
— Packaging and labeling our products so that consumers and users can make informed value judgments.
— Maintaining the highest advertising standards of integrity and good taste.
— Not engaging in bribery.

Share the profits of each local company with those who have contributed to its success, by:
— Rewarding employees through a profit sharing program.
— Allocating a share of the profits to enhance the well-being of communities where we operate.
— Developing better products and services for the benefit of consumers and users.
— Providing to shareholders a reasonable return on their investment.

Provide the general public with information about our activities so that they have a better understanding of our worldwide company.

We believe in contributing to the well-being of the countries and communities where we conduct business, and we commit ourselves to:

Seek actively the counsel and independent judgment of citizens of each country where we conduct business to provide guidance to local and corporate management, by:
— Selecting independent directors to serve on the board of each of our companies worldwide.
— Retaining distinguished associates and consultants to assist us in conducting our business according to the highest professional standards.

Contribute to the economic well-being of every country and community where we conduct business, by:
— Ensuring that new investment fits constructively into the economic development of each host country and local community.
— Encouraging the use of local suppliers and services offering competitive quality and prices.

Contribute to the social development of every country and community where we conduct business, by:
— Providing training programs for the development of skills.
— Staffing and managing with nationals from those countries wherever practicable.
— Involving ourselves in social, cultural, and educational projects which enhance the quality of life.

Be a good corporate citizen, by:
— Complying with and maintaining a due regard for the laws, regulations, and traditions of each country where we conduct business.

*We believe in improving international understanding,
and we commit ourselves to:*

**Act with responsible practices in international trade and
investment, by:**
— Retaining earnings necessary for reinvestment in our local
   companies and remitting dividends on a consistent basis.
— Making royalty, licensing, and service agreements which are fair and
   reasonable and which do not result in any hidden transfer of
   profits.
— Limiting foreign exchange transactions to normal business
   requirements and for the protection of our assets.

Promote the exchange of ideas and techniques, by:
— Encouraging the rapid diffusion of new technology to our local
   companies and licensees, while protecting our ownership rights and
   investment in such technology.
— Organizing worldwide and regional meetings for the dissemination
   and exchange of information.
— Providing support and assistance, especially in technical and
   professional fields, to develop skills throughout the organization.
— Following a balanced approach between transferring people to new
   jobs to gain experience and leaving people on the job long enough
   to make positive contributions in their assignments.
— Participating actively in non-political national and international
   activities with the objective of improving the global business climate.

THE ESSENCE OF A FAMILY ENTERPRISE

Designed by JMH Corporation

Composed by Weimer Typesetting in Baskerville

Printed by Hilltop Press